THE MERSEY SHIP REPAIRERS

Life and Work in a Port Industry

Kevin Moore

Docklands History Project
The University of Liverpool

First published by the Docklands
History Project 1988.
   Docklands History Project.

Cover design by Icon Graphic Design,
24 Hardman St, Liverpool.
L1 9AX.
Tel 051 709 3995

ISBN 0-9512107-2-6

Front cover photograph
George Taylor, shipwright at A & R Brown, caulking the deck of a ship, 1953

Back cover photograph:
Repairing the rudder of the *Glenstrae*, Brocklebank graving dock, June 1942.

Typeset in the University of Liverpool

Contents

Docklands History Project

The history of Merseyside is inseparable from the history of the people who lived and worked in the dockland areas. The Docklands History project exists to collect and preserve photographs, mementos and memories of life and industry in Merseyside so that a record of the dockland communities will be preserved for future generations.

We have produced portable exhibitions which have been shown in the Museum of Labour History, libraries, community centres and homes for the elderly. This pamphlet is the fourth in a series of studies of life and work in Merseyside's dockland communities. It follows *The Tapestry Makers: Life and Work at Lee's Tapestry Works, Birkenhead; The Liverpool Docklands: Life and Work in Athol Street;* and *Working the Tides: Gatemen and Masters on the River Mersey.* Most importantly, the project involves the community in the recovery and presentation of its own history. There are three project workers: Pat Ayers, Alan Johnson and Kevin Moore. For further information about the project please contact:

Docklands History Project
University of Liverpool
11 Abercromby Square
P.O. Box 147
LIVERPOOL. L69 3BX
Tel: 794-2408

Acknowledgements

Ship repair was one of Merseyside's main industries of the past, employing over 20,000 men and women at its peak in the 1940s. Yet almost nothing has been written about the history of this once great industry, or of the men and women who worked in it. As part of my work for the Docklands History Project, I have tried to rectify this. I began by appealing, in the local press, for ex-ship repairers to get in touch. The response was tremendous, over one hundred people making contact with offers of photographs, tools, union memorabilia, and most importantly, memories.

Wishing, but being unable to visit everyone, I decided to organise a reunion. On April 9th 1988 over 400 people gathered at Merseyside Maritime Museum in Albert Dock for an afternoon of memories of the ship repair industry. The event was largely for ex-workers from A & R Brown, and its associated companies, the firm I originally decided to focus upon. Brown's amalgamated with C & H Crichton in 1962, which later became CBS Engineering, before finally closing in 1980.

Ship repairers' reunion at the Maritime Museum
Photograph by Deepak Popli

However, there were ship repairers at the reunion from other famous local firms, such as Grayson Rollo and Harland Wolff.

This event touched a nerve with ex-ship repairers and their families. It evoked a widespread feeling that their working lives and sacrifices had been forgotten. As one woman, whose father worked in the industry for over fifty years, has written to me:

"Often I have noticed that these men have never been recognised as they should . . . Thank you for the remembrance of a vast army of workers".

I hope that this book will help to set the record straight, and acknowledge the key role played by these workers.

I am grateful to the Leverhulme Trust for the funding which has made this study possible. Thanks are also due to National Museums and Galleries on Merseyside and the University of Liverpool for their financial and professional support.

Alan Scarth and the staff of the Maritime Museum, Gordon Read and staff at the County Archives, and Janet Smith and staff at the Local History Record Office, Liverpool Central Library, have been as helpful as ever. I am also very grateful to Loraine Knowles, Curator of Merseyside Museum of Labour History, Harry Murt of the GMB, and Frank Lindstrom of Cammell Laird, for allowing me access to archives, and for giving advice and support. Many thanks to Ian Qualtrough and Susan Yee of the Photographic Unit at Liverpool University for all their excellent work. Thanks also to Paula McConville for the transcripts of the interview tapes, Patricia McMillan and Dianne Murgatroyd for typing the manuscript, and to Val Taylor for design and typesetting. My co-researchers on the Docklands History Project, Pat Ayers and Alan Johnson, and its directors, Tony Lane and Bob Lee, have all assisted me greatly. My thanks also to my co-worker, Gail Cameron, for supervising the production of this book.

Above all, I owe a great debt of thanks to all the ship repairers and their families who have given their help. This book simply could not have been put together without their contribution: to list all those who have loaned photographs, given memories or offered material for the exhibition would be impossible. I would like to offer my sincere thanks to you all. I am particularly grateful to Joe Cain, John Thompson, and John Waggott, three ship repairers who have given me invaluable assistance, by tracking down photographs, introducing me to old colleagues of theirs, and showing me what remains today of this once great industry.

Established 1853

A. RUTHERFORD & C.º LTD.

SHIPBUILDERS & REPAIRERS, ENGINEERS & BOILERMAKERS,
SHIP PAINTERS & DECORATORS.
Builders of
BARGES, STEAM & MOTOR LAUNCHES, TUGS, ETC.

1.   Ship Repair

"A morning mist darkened the grey churning ocean, but the little tramp steamer pushed stubbornly ahead. Up and down she pitched in the hissing foam of a storm-roused sea. As her bow dipped under water one tumbling wave bashed against it in full force, shook the suspended anchors, and entirely swamped the forecastle head. With a quivering heave it rose again to send a swash of cascading streams pouring below to the well-deck. Then down plunged the bow once more as another sheet of water, rushing inboard, swept the cowl of a ventilator clattering along the deck, excited the bridge-officer's whistle, and jerked a cursing sailor out of his forecastle daydream."

(Extract from the short story *Fishmeal* by Merseyside seaman George Garrett)

The sea is a constant hazard to shipping and working at sea remains the most dangerous of all occupations. While most ships safely return to their home port, they have always suffered general wear and tear, and usually some more serious form of damage. The weather will always be the greatest danger at sea, but there are also the hazards of collision, fire and explosion, of squeezing into a dock through narrow entrances, of handling cumbersome items of cargo, of cargo shifting or breaking loose at sea.

Let us envisage the scene when a ship came into Liverpool in the late 1940's, in the heyday of the ship repair industry. A ship manager from the firm that usually carried out the repairs on that ship would come down to receive instructions. If the hull or the propellers needed attention, shipwrights would guide the ship into one of Merseyside's nineteen dry docks, where the ship would be propped upright and the water pumped out. Scores of workers in a host of different trades would then commence work. Fitters would go to the engine room, boilermakers repair the boilers, scalers clean out the insides of the boilers and water tanks. Shipwrights and joiners would set to work checking, repairing and replacing wooden fittings, whether it was hatchboards, the lifeboats, or down in the cargo holds. Blacksmiths would begin work on anchors, cables, derricks and guard-rails. Plumbers would be repairing pipework in the hold of a refrigerated ship. Riveters, burners and welders could be working on shell plating, superstructure or rails.

Aerial view of Grayson Rollo and Clover's graving docks, Birkenhead, 1960
Loaned by John Waggott

There would also be coppersmiths and tinsmiths, riggers, painters, electricians, cleaners and a large number of general labourers assisting the skilled tradesmen. Alongside many of the tradesmen were young apprentices learning the craft, perhaps mesmerised by their first time in an engine room or in a graving dock. If the ship was a passenger or cargo liner upholsterers and french polishers would also be on board. The repair firm would also have premises along the dock road, with a workshop for each trade, where items from the ship could be taken for repair.

Ship repairers were highly skilled workers. In most of the twenty or so different trades, a five-year apprenticeship had to be served, between the ages of 16 and 21, before becoming a fully-qualified tradesman. This was to a large extent a man's world. Nearly all the trades were the sole preserve of men. Women did work in the industry in significant numbers, but they were restricted to those jobs which have traditionally been seen as part of a 'woman's role': cleaning the ships and undertaking the sewing work in upholstery.

While after each voyage a ship would usually need some repairs (traditionally known as a 'haircut and shave') a ship also had to have regular checks against general wear and tear, whether due to the corrosive effects of sea water, or the strain years of use placed on cables, winches and derricks. Annual, triannual and four yearly overhauls were required for both insurance purposes and to pass Board of Trade standards. These were carried out by ship repair firms. The firms also undertook a great deal of modernisation work, such as switching ships from coal fuel to oil-burning. There was also the conversion work, during the Second World War, of altering ships for military requirements—and reconversion back to civilian usage after the war. Modernisation or conversion work could keep a ship in dry dock for several months, whereas voyage repairs might be completed within a matter of days, while the ship was being unloaded and loaded with cargo.

Ship repair on Merseyside is as old as the port itself. Shipbuilding had effectively died out in Liverpool by the 1850's, the growth of the docks forcing the main firms over to the Birkenhead shore. However, with so many ships entering the rapidly expanding Liverpool docks, ship repair flourished. H & C Grayson, founded in the 1750's, was originally a shipbuilding firm, but came to specialise in repairs. By the 1950's Grayson's had become the largest ship repair firm in the world. This was partly through taking over or amalgamating, with other local firms, such as Rollo's, Clover's, Clayton's and R & J Evans. Apart from the extensive main workshops at Sandhills Grayson's had smaller shops in the South End, Garston and Birkenhead.

HMS Vanguard in a Liverpool graving dock, probably during the First World War
Loaned by Joe Cain

A & R Brown was founded in 1837 and initially the firm specialised in copper and brass work. It was not until the First World War that the firm became one of the most important general repair firms. In 1913 Harland and Wolff, the Belfast shipbuilders, opened a ship repair shop in Bootle, by the Brocklebank graving dock. This was soon one of the largest local firms, employing 4,800 within a year. Other major ship repair firms on the Liverpool side of the river were C & H Crichton (founded 1880), J. Russell (founded 1889), Charles Howson, J. A. Mulhern, Archibald Brown, and J. W. Pickering.

In Birkenhead, Cammell Laird have long been a major ship repair firm, as well as shipbuilders, but there were other smaller firms such as J. Gordon Alison, A. Rutherford & Co, and William Cubbin Ltd. Many of the major shipping lines operating from Liverpool also had extensive workshops at one time. There were a host of other small firms, particularly before the war: in the 1920's there were over 80 firms in the Mersey Ship Repairers Employers' Federation.

The Mersey Docks and Harbour Board also had extensive workshops for the upkeep of its own vessels and owned 19 of the port's 'graving' or 'dry' docks, which it leased out to the various ship repair companies on a day-to-day basis. Grayson's, however owned five of their own graving docks in Birkenhead, and Cammell Laird a further seven. Few of Merseyside's graving docks are still in operation.

Gladstone graving dock, December 1962
Source: Liverpool Daily Post and Echo

Not all the ship repair firms were 'complete', in the sense that they had workshops for every trade. Harland and Wolff employed all the trades; Grayson's however, lacked an upholstery shop; A & R Brown relied on joiners from its associated company, Mersey Insulation. Other firms specialised in just one aspect of ship repair, such as James Troop (pipe fabrication and the reconditioning of marine fuel injection equipment), Campbell and Isherwood (electrical engineers) and F.M. Porter Ltd (scalers). These would be contracted by the shipowner for one part of a repair job. Even the general ship repair firms had specialisms, which enabled them to do general engineering work away from ship repair. A & R Brown, for example, specialised in copper and brass work, and undertook a great deal of work for Tate and Lyle.

Most of the firms had begun as family firms, and some like Troop's remained so. Others, however, were bought out by shipping companies. A & R Brown was taken over by Houlder Brothers; Ellerman's largely owned C & H Chrichton; Charles Howson's was controlled by Cunard. Most of the repair work these firms undertook was on the ships of their parent companies. These shipping lines thereby ensured that their ships would always be repaired as a priority, and valuable time would not be lost. Other ship repair firms, though not owned by a shipping line, tended to be given work by one in particular. Harland's, for example, repaired ships built at the Belfast yard, largely White Star liners.

There were still 10,000 workers employed in ship repair on Merseyside in 1961. The region was the second most important

Harland and Wolff's Bootle Works, 1939. Note the Overhead Railway in the foreground
Source: Ulster Folk and Transport Museum Photographic Archive, Harland and Wolff Collection

centre of ship repair in the country after London, employing over a quarter of all those in the industry in Britain as a whole. Today, only a few hundred ship repairers are employed on Merseyside, by a handful of small firms.

This dramatic collapse of the industry locally cannot be understood in isolation. The industry has sharply declined across the country. In turn this is a reflection of the startling reduction in the size of Britain's merchant fleet: from 3,300 ships in 1950 to 940 in 1984. There are simply far fewer ships to repair. A higher percentage of Britain's trade is carried in foreign ships.

Changes in ship technology and design have also reduced the amount of repair work required. The smaller number of ships entering British ports generally each need less repairs. The passenger liners have gone, killed off by the aeroplane. These floating hotels, with their highly complex layouts and ornate furnishings, created a great deal of work for ship repairers. The cargo liners have also disappeared in the last twenty years. The container ships which have replaced them are far simpler in design, like floating warehouses, and thus tend to require less repair work. These ships do not have their own cargo-handling gear to be repaired, while the old six-hatch ship had twenty derricks, with as many winches.

Since the 1960s shipping companies have stepped up a policy of getting crews to do as much repairs at sea as possible, and have introduced planned maintenance. Seamen were traditionally only expected to do cleaning and painting, but they now have to use portable welding, burning and grit-blasting equipment. They can do small repairs around the ship which used to be left until the return to port. This is a double saving for the shipping companies: the turnaround times in port are cut, and they get more for their money from the seamen's labour.

Yet it has to be recognised that the ship repair industry has declined more dramatically in Merseyside than in other parts of the country. This is a reflection of the particularly acute decline of Liverpool as a port. In 1966 Liverpool was still the second largest UK port; by 1985 it was sixth. The concentration of industry, population and wealth in the south-east of the country has benefitted the ports of that region at the expense of Liverpool. The decline of Commonwealth countries as trading partners and the rise of the EEC nations has effectively left Liverpool marooned on the wrong side of the country. The particularly dramatic collapse of the ship repair industry on Merseyside has been an inevitable consequence of the especially acute decline of the port.

2. Ship Repairers

For boys growing up in the dockland areas of Merseyside there have always been only a small number of possible jobs on leaving school. What made a young lad become a ship repairer, rather than a seaman, a docker, or a worker in the food-processing industries? It was largely the accident of birth which decided who worked in ship repair. Traditionally, sons followed their fathers into the industry, usually in the same trade. The result was that large numbers of different generations of the same family worked in the same trade at the same firm. Bob Morrison recalls of A & R Brown, "It was a family firm. Practically everyone had someone related there. I got there because of my father". According to Joyce Thompson, wages clerk at Brown's,

> "On the wages there would be the same name coming up time and time again, and they tended to stay in the same trade. There would be a lot of one name in the scalers, a lot of Mulhollands and a lot of McGraths. The Dixon family, Jack Dixon was foreman tinsmith and his son-in-law worked in the tin shop but his son was a turner. Yes, there were fathers and sons. I think that was well known on the dock as a whole, all parts of the dock estate, both the dockers and the firms, families tended to stay, the father would get the son a job. You'd come across the same name time and time again when you were making up the wages."

Dave Langton jokes of his family connection with Cubbin's in Birkenhead over the years:

> "They nearly changed the name of William Cubbin Ltd. to

Langton-Langton and Son because my dad was the boss rigger, my uncle was a wagon driver, my other uncle was a diver cum rigger and I was an apprentice fitter... Then you had the Mottleys, the father, two brothers, the cousins were all scalers, and the sons were apprentice fitters, all close knit."

Page from a C & H Crichton brochure, 1959, demonstrating the strong connections of one family with the firm
Loaned by Joe Duffy

Few ship repairers recall, however, that it was their childhood ambition to follow in their father's footsteps. The exceptions were those who wanted to become fitters, but for them the motivation was the adventure of going to sea, since this was the usual step on completion of a fitter's apprenticeship. For many of these lads going to sea was 'in the blood', and also a tradition of the area they grew up in. Dave Langton recalls growing up in Wallasey:

> "My dad was a seaman, 21 years at sea, an AB Quartermaster with Blue Funnel Line... Where I was born and bred, most of the fella's in the street were all in the merchant navy. Someone in the street was always away at sea, and when he came home all the kids in the street benefitted. Like my old uncle Douglas, when he came home, everyone in the street used to be round our house, nice as pie, and he'd have a big box of Wrigley's chewies. So it was a thing, they all went away to sea somehow, that was just in our street."

But the desire to go to sea in Dave Langton's case, as in many others, was tempered by his father's insistence that you had "got to get a trade behind you" first, and so he became an apprentice fitter at Cubbin's in Birkenhead.

If becoming a fitter and going to sea was glamorous, few saw the other ship repair trades in the same light. Other lads were forced into the trade of their fathers, often despite other ambitions. Sometimes a lad's ambition was almost certainly unattainable, such as becoming a draughtsman; more often, a father had to oppose a son's desire to take up a 'glamorous' and 'well paid' job as a telegraph boy or a delivery boy of some kind. However, most boys left school at 14, and usually they could only begin an apprenticeship when they were 16, so to begin with parents would accept their taking these kinds of jobs. The arguments began when sons did not want to give up their 'glamorous' jobs. This reluctance was partly because they would be paid so much less as an apprentice. As Arthur Robinson recalls of his milk delivery job in the 1930's:

> "I was getting 16 shillings a week when I was in the co-op at 15. I would have got a rise to 21 shillings when I was 16 but I left, and it was a big drop, from 16s to 5s wasn't it! My ma got nothing out of me, because it used to cost four shillings to get to work and the other shilling was pocket money."

To most young lads of 16 the prospect of keeping the much higher wage must have seemed far more financially attractive than the idea of serving a five-year apprenticeship.

Coppersmiths at Fawcett and Preston Ltd., Liverpool, about 1935. Left to right: Joseph Robinson, ?, Bob Bradley, George Merrin
Loaned by Arthur Robinson

In many cases, particularly in the 1930's, when such a large number of men were unemployed for long periods, the family could not afford to allow a son to serve an apprenticeship even if he was lucky enough to get one, because they were so dependent on the extra money. However, if a father decided that his son was to take up an apprenticeship, there was no room for argument, as Bob Maguire recalls:

> "I left school when I was 14, in 1920. I first went to work in Buddin's in Lime Street, a well-known chemist ... Dr. Buddin wanted me to carry on and be a chemist. He thought I had the ability and he wanted to pay for me to be a chemist and I wanted to be one. But in those days you did what your father told you to do. That was it, 'you're going to be a shipwright and that's that'."

Often, however, there was no need for an argument because employers chose to sack boys in such jobs at 16, when they would start having to pay a stamp (national insurance) for them, and preferred to take on another 14 year old. Some lads, however, needed no encouragement to take up an apprenticeship. They saw the long-term benefits of having a trade from the experience of the likes of elder brothers. As Leslie I'Anson recollects:

> "My brother was an engineer at sea, with the Canadian Pacific Line. And out of the family, there were four brothers, he seemed to be the most affluent, and I often thought that if I was going to make anything of myself I'd have to have a trade."

Most sons were ultimately willing to follow the wishes of the father because, particularly before the Second World War, they had precious little chance of finding another job by themselves. The influence a father could wield at his own workplace was crucial in getting a son an apprenticeship. Bob Maguire speaks of how his father got him an apprenticeship as a shipwright with Lampert and Holt:

> "He was the foreman porter there, my grandfather had been there before him. Your family fixed you up. It was like you had to have a messsage from the Angel Gabriel to get a job as an apprentice ... Family connections helped everybody."

If a father could not pull strings to get a son an apprenticeship, an uncle might be able to. In John Rock's case, as an upholsterer, it was an aunt in the trade who used her influence on his behalf:

> "I went to A & R Brown's, I got the job because the

Joseph Robinson, coppersmith, who served his apprenticeship at A & R Brown,
1899-1906, at his home in Dyson Street.
Loaned by Arthur Robinson

foreman Mr. Bill Johnson was a friend of my aunt Margaret, they served their apprenticeship in the same shop, Waring and Gillows, before the 1914-18 war."

It was still possible, if less likely, to be able to get into ship repair without a family connection. Ken Patterson recalls that the word of a neighbour who was a patternmaker at A & R Brown was good enough to get him an apprenticeship there in that trade in the 1940s. For those without even the most tenuous link of this kind, trying to get an apprenticeship in the 1930's could be a fruitless task. Leslie I'Anson was only successful through great persistence, combined with a good educational ability, and an element of good fortune. His first job was as an errand boy with Burn's the jewellers in Bold Street, Liverpool. He realised that at 16 they would sack him and take on a 14 year old, so that they did not have to pay national insurance. So Leslie used his half-day off to call at all the ship repair firms on the dock road, seeking an apprenticeship as an electrical engineer:

"The answer was always the same... that they hadn't enough work for the men, let alone young boys, and they weren't taking apprentices. And of course this was at the slough of the depression, 1933. Eventually I was 17, almost going on for 18, that would be 1934, when I went into C & H Crichton on Derby Road, I'd been in there many many times. Again I asked to see the chief clerk, and he came to the counter in the reception area. He said: 'I don't really know why you keep coming here because the answer is the same'. I said: 'My father says things can change day by day and there is always a possibility'. At that moment who should walk through that reception area but the joint manager, Mr. Tommy West. He said 'what does this young man want?' The chief clerk said 'he's been coming here for a long, long time asking for a job as an apprentice and I keep telling him there isn't enough work for the men let alone boys.' Mr. West said to me: 'Come into my office and we'll have a chat'. He asked me questions such as what I did at school. 'Did you do geometry'? 'Yes' I said 'I did geometry'. So he asked me 'What is a triangle?' I said 'It's a three sided figure. I know that there are 3 types of triangles, scalene, equalateral and isosceles'. He said 'Can you explain what a circle is?' I said 'If you give me a pair of compasses I can draw you a circle'. He said 'Any fool can do that, can you explain?' I was intelligent enough to know that he wanted a sort of explanation of what a circle was, so I said 'If I can't answer you correctly perhaps if I told you that I'd be prepared to go to nightschool and maybe after the first season I'd be able to tell you.' He said 'that's the spirit boy, you can start next Monday as an apprentice marine engine fitter' at the princely sum of 5/- 6d a week."

C & H Crichton employees, 1937, taken in front of the machine shop. Leslie I'Anson is on the far right of the back row.
Loaned by Leslie I'Anson

He did go to nightschool, and discovered the definition of a circle, and learned it off by heart in case Mr. West ever asked—which he did a few months later!

George Conroy, though he also had no one to speak for him, also found that a good education was enough to get him an apprenticeship:

"I used to go to a technical school, Walton Technical School in Carisbrooke Road, Liverpool. We did quite a bit of machine drawing, trigonometry and metal work, all that sort of stuff...I had to write around to different firms from the school, different firms looking for apprentices".

He got a place at William Beardmore's as an apprentice blacksmith, and not as engineer as he had hoped, but this was still a great relief:

"Jobs were few and far between in those days, 1929, 1930. Those were the days when it was quite common to see children running around the streets in their bare feet, winter and summer. I was glad of a job in any case."

Unless, like George, you won a scholarship to technical college (and these were few and far between), the fees were beyond the reach of most working-class people. Even scholarship winners incurred expense in terms of materials for school such as pens and pencils. In some cases, families could not afford to let scholarship winners attend. It was only a few relatively prosperous working-class families that could ensure that their sons had the benefit of such an education.

While 'who you know' will always remain a factor in how people get jobs, by the 1960s getting an apprenticeship in ship repair became less dependent on personal contacts. George Conroy, by then foreman blacksmith at A & R Brown, explains:

"Lads wanting jobs weren't allowed to come to the firms to enquire about them. The schools they went to would get in touch with you, ask you did you want any apprentices. You'd tell them what you had available and then they would allocate so many boys. The lads would come to the firm and be interviewed by the general manager."

In the skilled ship repairing trades, lads were traditionally bound as apprentices to a firm for seven, but later five and more recently four, years. Before the start of an apprenticeship the thought of entering a ship repair yard filled youngsters with a mixture of trepidation and excitement. The reality was sometimes a disappointment particularly for those who had been taken on before their 16th birthday, before they could actually begin their apprenticeship. As Ken Patterson, a patternmaker at A & R Brown, recalls:

"You weren't allowed to use the woodworking machinery just in case you whipped your finger off. So you made the tea, ran the messages, went into the dock canteen for the toast for them, brushed the shop up, because we didn't have a labourer in our shop... When you started to serve your time when you were sixteen you still carried on in the same mould. It used to get a bit boring at times, half past eleven, you're going to make the tea!"

Equally a part of beginning an apprenticeship was being the butt of good natured jokes: "When you first started they used to send you to somebody else for a long stand or a left-handed spanner." Or Question: Where does the last rivet go in a ship? Answer: In the last hole! If all can remember this kind of initiation, not all recollect an initiation of a more physical kind. But this tradition was still very much alive at Cubbin's in the 1950's, as Dave Langton recalls:

"If the chippies (shipwrights) were working on a barge and you had to go down into the hold of the barge to look up at the beams, to get the tonnage, you'd shout down to the chippies, can you tell me what it is? 'Come down and get it', and there'd be four or five chippies down there putting a new ceiling in the barge. You knew very well what would happen to you if you went down there! Initiation ceremony, they'd have you: 'We haven't had this one'. It was wicked. They'd sort of spread eagle you on the deck and nail big nails to your boiler suit, and leave you there. I've known fellas be there half a day. At five o'clock at night when the shipyard had gone quite, all the machines had knocked off, you'd hear someone shouting and screaming!"

Dave also recalls an initiation amongst his own trade, the fitters:

"They'd put your arms and legs in the vices and then down came the tea leaves and the grease, they'd leave you like that. Oh wicked, the initiation ceremonies. It was all part of growing up in a ship yard, make or break you."

If such experiences can be recalled with a smile now, at the time some clearly found them disturbing, particularly as in some cases they bordered on the sadistic. As one joiner remembers:

"One of the things they used to do was put paint on your private parts. Just after I left they did it to another. When he went home his mother saw the paint on his underclothes and his father asked him what had happened. The father went straight to the police and the whole lot were held for indecent assault."

The older apprentices were generally to the fore in the initiations; and new boys could also expect to end up in fights provoked by the older lads. As a coppersmith recalls:

"Just my luck the fella I had to fight was a great big lad and I was only small. He knocked hell out of me, but you've got to accept it. And then, of course, your initiation, they got you and stripped you down, red-leaded you! You had to go through all these things, you just laughed them off, because you did the same later on. There was no pity anywhere."

Apprentices at Hugh Douglas & Co. Jamaica Street, Liverpool 1955
Loaned by Don McKee, who is third from the left on the back row

Apprenticeship could be a testing time, particularly in the depression of the 1930s, when the father and other members of the family could be out of work. An apprentice's wages were very low, from as little as five shillings a week for a first-year apprentice. As a fitter recalls:

"Occasionally you'd have a penny, perhaps you hadn't come on your bike that day because you'd got a puncture, and you'd got a penny for the tram home. Another apprentice would come along and say 'have you got a penny?' 'Well, yes I've got a penny, its the fare home, what do you want it for?' 'I want to buy a packet of woodbines'. So you had 2½ woodbines, you got 5 for tuppence, 2½ woodbines for a penny, and you walked home!"

For those without the support of a family the life could be very grim. A welder recalls that as an apprentice in the 1930s he lived in a bedsit in Admiral Street, Liverpool 8:

"It was just a bed, a table, and a cooker in the corner, and I bought a second hand radio from somewhere. It was just basic. No carpet, just oilcloth on the floor. In winter you had to ruffle yourself up with clothes to keep warm when you went to bed... You walked to work, you couldn't afford tram fares. Most days it was bread and jam, sometimes you could afford perhaps a lamb chop or something like that, fish and chips was a luxury. You had to darn your socks and when the hole got too big that it wouldn't take darn you put a patch in. You just existed. Bad times, you were just on the border line of thieving to live".

One way for an apprentice to make a little extra money was to make tools to sell:

"You'd go in the scrap and find a piece of metal and you'd make tools, and someone would come along and say 'how much do you want for that?' You were so short of money you'd say 'is half a crown too much?' Sometimes you'd spend hours and hours and hours making it, and they'd give you a shilling for it."

Despite their poverty apprentices would always do their best to 'look the part', by wearing the right sort of cap:

"I used to buy mine from Lewis's. Some of them got them from relatives who'd been to sea. You'd notice that some of them were bigger, those were the ones that were the pukka thing they used at sea. If their fathers or their brothers had a spare one they'd give it to them. I think they were half a crown, but always, if you were an apprentice, you had to be dressed like an apprentice."

Not all ship repairers entered the industry as apprentices. Riggers were usually men who had served many years at sea as ABs and who were then looking for a shore job. Many of these were fascinating old characters to the young apprentices. Bob Maguire recalls of Lamport and Holts:

"We had a chap called Jack Scoburth, he was the storekeeper, a Russian Finn. That man had cut his own leg off at sea. When you come to look at the condition of the ships: they were steered by a chain going along the deck, and this chain had carried away and wrapped itself round his leg, but he amputated his own leg at sea. He was a wonderful man."

Men with relevant skills could also move into ship repair from the general engineering industry, as could painters and plumbers from housebuilding and construction. And, of course, many who served their apprenticeships as *shipbuilders* at Cammell Laird elected to work instead in ship repair. In the 1920's, when there was a shortage of labour locally, many Belfast men were brought over to work at Harland's and Laird's, and at least some settled permanently on Merseyside. But on the whole ship repair was a 'family business'.

Aside from the lack of a family connection, there were other factors which lessened a youngster's chances of getting a job in the industry. Women were traditionally excluded from all jobs in ship repair except cleaning and upholstery. A shortage of labour in the industry in the Second World War did, however, slightly increase the openings for women. A few women came into the workshops of several ship repair firms, to work on such jobs as drilling. One such woman was Amy Beattie, who after losing her husband in the war, got a job as a steam hammer operator in the blacksmiths shop at Rutherford's in Birkenhead:

"I think the men were a little bit dubious at first, wondering if I would be able to cope with it, but I did. I've always been a fighter, I've had to be."

Though a few women had worked in the offices of ship repair firms before the war, their numbers were now vastly increased, as the male office workers were called up. Joyce Thompson recalls how, as a sixteen year old who had just left school, it was quite a shock to enter the very male world of a ship repair firm, in her case A & R Brown:

"It was quite a rough environment, my vocabulary doubled in the first three months! It must have been quite an upheaval when the women started coming in. The time office I imagine would have been almost as tough as in the shop until the women came. They had to moderate their language and their behaviour, not that it was moderated all that much!"

At the end of the war, however, most of the women lost their jobs in favour of men returning from the services. Both Joyce Thompson and Amy Beattie were very fortunate to be kept on,

Amy Beattie and others from the blacksmiths' shop at A Rutherford & Co., Birkenhead, about 1944
Loaned by Amy Beattie

Amy keeping her job in the blacksmiths shop: "The boss just went into the office and said 'She's not going because we want her here' . . . The chap whose job I took, he came back and the boss gave him a job as a striker."

Religion, particularly before the Second World War, did play some part in a person's ability to get a job in the industry, though such discrimination seems to have taken place rather subtly. Certainly Harland and Wolff were seen as a firm which favoured Protestants; and one man recalls that: "there was a firm that wouldn't take you on in the upholstery department if you weren't a Catholic." Discrimination against black and Chinese ship repairers has always been even more clear-cut. A foreman recalls that he was given an abusive nickname by the men when he took on several black welders. Another man recalls that Chinese fitters were only taken on when everyone else had a job. There was one other notable form of discrimination, against trade unionists. Ernie Parker recalls that for a considerable period he found it difficult to get a job as a moulder because of his prominence in the moulders' union:

"They could start a moulder the next day or half an hour afterwards, but the particular time I went they just didn't need a moulder. This was what was said to my union. And victimisation is a very hard thing to prove, because all they used to say was they didn't need anyone at that particular time...I suffered badly through my union activity."

3. Work

Out on the ships

Many of the trades in ship repair were based largely in the workshops; others, such as the shipwrights, spent almost all of their time out on the ships. Of the twenty or so skilled trades in ship repair, the shipwright could lay claim to be the oldest, but with the switch to metal hulls, new trades, particularly the plater, began to take over much of the shipwright's work. (See front cover photograph). The shipwright eventually came to be responsible only for work in wood, and wood was being used less and less on ships. Even so, this still involved a fair amount of regular repair work, from overhauling the lifeboats, to replacing hatch covers, to repairing masts, blocks, and pulleys. The shipwright was also originally responsible for all the wood work involved in the insulation of the holds of ships, and for making furnishings such as doors, tables and cupboards, though increasingly this work was being taken over by ships' joiners. The caulking of wooden decks was also originally a large part of the shipwright's work. (See front cover photograph). Caulking was not a popular part of the work: "That was a terrible job. You'd have to do 144 feet and three seams in, with your caulking mallet, and then pitch it, for a day's work. Nobody ever volunteered for that job." Some men developed a way of only having to put two layers of oakum in instead of three:

"Fellas got a special tool made. They'd have a caulking iron cut and twisted, so that when it went in the seam it'd stick some of the oakum into the timber on each side, the oakum wouldn't be right down, so there'd only be two threads of oakum in."

The switch to metal decks meant that this kind of work was also lost to the shipwrights, though ocean liners, for aesthetic reasons, continued to have wooden decks covering a metal one.

The other major responsibility of the shipwrights was the bringing of ships into dry dock for repairs. Before a ship came in, the foreman shipwright would consult the plans of the ship, and supervise the arrangement of wooden blocks on which the keel would sit. Small ships or those with a broad keel could sit on these blocks without further support. Most often, however, pitch pine poles, from 10 feet to 40 feet long, had to be put between the sides of the ship and the stepped graving dock walls, to act as props to keep the ship upright. As the water was gradually removed from the dock, the shores were gradually levered into position by the shipwrights, with the aid of labourers. Once all the water had been removed, repair work could begin on the hull of the ship.

Docking (and undocking) was a much sought after part of a shipwright's work:

"For a docking, you got paid for a day no matter how long it took you. If you did it in half a day, you got a day's pay; about four hours was the most it ever took. You were lucky if you got picked, that was one of the plums of the job, you only had to carry a maul around, nothing else. Other times you had to carry the tool box weighing a hundred weight around."

While each firm employed its own shipwrights, there was also a 'pool' of shipwrights in Liverpool who were hired specifically for docking. They had the advantage of not having to keep up their tools, and made good money in a short time. The disadvantage was that they had to wait their turn for another docking job, which might mean several days without work.

The switch from wood to iron and later steel as the main material used in ship construction led the boilermakers to overtake the shipwrights as the premier trade in both building and repair. However, it is misleading to describe 'boilermaker' as a trade, since it is made up of several specialisms: the boilermaker proper, who actually works on the construction, overhaul and repair of ship's boilers; platers; burners, who use oxygen cutting equipment; and riveters and welders. From the Second World War onwards

Grayson Rollo welding plant attendant at work in the docks, 1950's.
Loaned by John Waggott

riveting was gradually being replaced by welding in ship construction, and therefore repair, and by the 1960's it was a largely redundant technique.

Naturally the overhaul or repair of a ship's engines was an important part of the industry. Some fitters specialised in working in the machine shop, but most worked almost all the time out on the ships. Each fitter, through experience, came to specialise in different types of engines, and tended to be given the same kind of work. Electricians were also an important trade out on the ships, maintaining the wide variety of electrical equipment, and providing temporary working lights for scalers and other trades. Ship's plumbers also had a large range of work, on passenger ships and crew accommodation in particular, but also on ship's insulation.

Out on the ships there were also a wide range of less skilled labouring jobs in which no apprenticeship was served. Chief among these were the scalers. Tom Fairbrother recalls his first day as a scaler, just after the Second World War:

"We had to go down into the fresh water tanks and chip all the old cement wash off with a hammer. They were hard to get into because you had to climb through openings like portholes without the glass, it was very awkward. When you finished chipping away you put all the old cement in a bucket and sent it through. The man at the far end would pass through buckets of fresh cement wash and we'd brush decks, sides and the bulk-head, and then move out to another tank ... The crawling was the hardest part. The tanks were only a few feet high, so that you had to work in a bent over position like Quasimodo, the Hunchback of Notre Dame".

The conditions were as dark as they were claustrophobic, with only candles at this time providing light. But the worst aspect of the job was the dirt, especially when cleaning out oil tanks:

"When you were doing the oil tanks, there was no such thing as protective clothing then, you just went in the way you were. It was crude oil, and it used to cling and smell. When I got home I had to take my clothes off on the step, wrap them up and then just go in the way I was. My mother would have a bath ready. There was no such thing as launderettes then, you just had to clean them the best way you could. Of course she didn't have a washing machine, so they had to be done in the bath. When she was done I had to clean the oil off the bath.

When you worked on oil tankers you'd get what they called time and fifty. If you worked 8 hours in an oil tanker you'd get paid for 12 hours. The money was obviously for the damage that it was doing to your clothes, because you'd only need four jobs on an oil tanker and you'd have to throw them away, the crude oil used to rot them".

Scalers were also employed to clean out the sewage tanks on the passenger liners. In summer scaling was particularly unpleasant, the men having to work semi-naked in a hot, stuffy atmosphere. As one man recalls:

> "If it was a good summer I always went on the building, I preferred to work on the building rather than the stinking confines of a ship. Because believe me some of them did smell. You'd get a lot of fellas including myself who couldn't be bothered going ashore or using the toilet on the top deck!"

Scalers taking a break from work, about 1900
Loaned by Matthew Dillon

Painters and riggers were two other important trades in which no apprenticeship was served. There were also labourers who worked alongside skilled tradesmen, such as with fitters and shipwrights. There were 'box-keepers', men who looked after the stores and tools for each trade out on the ships. There were also what were known as 'runners', men like Jack Lawler or Jimmy Thompson at A & R Brown, as Joyce Thompson recalls:

"If a chargehand or foreman down on the ship wanted something in a hurry and couldn't wait for it until the next day, he would send a man back to the office or back to the shop in the main building to say that he wanted so many of such and such. Or maybe he wanted five more workmen or he wanted five more labourers, the runner would come back with the message. Mind you they didn't run all the way, they used to use the public transport. Even if Liverpool would have been booming there job would have gone because they obviously would use two-way radio now. They knew the dock road and the docks like the backs of their hands, and they knew which ship was in which dock and for how long, they were a mountain of information. They were worth every penny, though they were just paid labourers wages."

There were also drivers, such as Dick and Bob Fitzgerald and Ronnie Mann at A & R Brown, who moved heavier equipment to and from the ships. The women ship's cleaners, though also 'unskilled', were an important part of ship repair, not least because they did all the cleaning work preparatory for painting.

Overall responsibility for the carrying out of repairs on a particular ship lay with a ship manager. Sometimes work was allocated directly by the ship owner to the general manager of the ship repair firm, but more usually the ship manager would have to go down to the ship, and speak to the captain, chief engineer and stewards about what work was required. He would then pass on this information to a cost clerk: each kind of repair job on a ship had a job number and was pre-costed, and so the cost clerk could thus immediately begin to work on the account. The ship manager would then allocate the number of men from each trade needed to work on the ship, and was responsible for 'keeping them on their toes' on the job. On the completion of repairs he would pass on information to the cost clerk regarding labour and material costs, and then check the final account. The cost clerks' final account, as John Thompson of A & R Brown recalls,

"could run into 10, 20, 30 pages of description of a big ship, a big overhaul being done. You'd describe everything in detail from the engineering point of view. Then you would put your hours worked by all the different trades, then your material, total them all up and add your ECs, which was your establish charges, which was $37\frac{1}{2}$ per cent, then your profit which could be 5 or 10 per cent depending on the company, and you could give a discount of $2\frac{1}{2}$ depending on the company ... We all had our own particular companys to do, I

Teddy London, rigger, working on the six inch circ. talurit splicing machine, C & H
Crichton, 1958
Loaned by Joe Duffy

dealt with sundry firms and steamers. George Barlow dealt with
Furness Withy and Royal Mail. Another man would do Shaw Savill
and Albion and another would do New Zealand Shipping

Company. You stuck with those companies, you dealt with the ships of those companies year after year."

Preparing an account and receiving payment were often two very different things. John Thompson, again:

"the English ships you were dealing with, say Houlder Brothers, Furness Withy, Pacific Steam Navigation, Royal Mail Line, Lamport & Holt, they all paid of course, monthly by cheque. But occasionally you'd get a small foreign ship come for repairs, a Greek, an Indian, an Italian, which was owned very often by the Captain. Before that ship sailed you'd have to get your money in cash, otherwise you never saw him again... Maybe the job had only been done in the morning and by early afternoon you'd have produced the invoice, all the detailed cost and everything and you'd go down to the ship, go on board, demand to see the Captain in his cabin. You'd demand the money off him. Very often he would 'hum and huh' and try to get away with it, and if he could he'd go to sea without paying. And then if he finally did agree to pay it, he'd want a backhander. You had to cope with characters like that."

Directly responsible to the ship managers, there would be a foreman in each trade. He was responsible for the allocation of men to particular jobs, ensuring that the necessary equipment was delivered to each ship, that the men received equal overtime—and for the hiring and firing of men. This was not a job that was necessarily desired, as George Conroy recalls of the late 1940's:

"I didn't know whether I wanted to be the foreman, because being the foreman you became one of the staff and you came onto a fixed wage. Of course there was a lot of overtime about in those days, we were working seven days a week, from 7.30 in the morning until 9.00 at night. But it was a case of either take it or leave it, if you didn't take the foreman's job you were up the road, so I had to take it. I probably lost money on it in the first year or two but the overtime petered out, and the foreman's wages and conditions got a lot better."

A good technical education was essential to being chosen as a foreman, but as one man recalls, there was probably another necessary qualification:

"I possibly had the bearing. I didn't seem to lark around like the other lads did. I've been told this later. In my younger days, if I went into a pub the manager would say to me 'who are you looking for?' I'd say 'No one in particular, why?' They used to think I was a detective! Because I had this trilby on and always a short haircut."

Foremen always liked to look the part:

"Of course all the foremen at Grayson Rollo's were always well dressed, always had a nice suit on. The reason for that was we used to go to a little tailors shop in Great Homer Street which used to have orders that had not been picked up, so we used to purchase these things cheap, or slight seconds. We'd go and buy a brand new suit off him for a pound or so. And, of course, we always wore a trilby. The foreman rigger always wore a brown velour trilby, quite a big rim, very proud of it, he was a character in his own right, fella named George Dunbell. George had to have a better trilby than anyone else!"

Repairing the rudder of the *Glenstrae*, Brocklebank graving dock, June 1942
Source: Merseyside Maritime Museum

Under the foremen were chargehands. Their responsibilities varied with the size of the firm. At the smaller firms, where foremen could get to all the jobs, chargehands did little more than order materials and tools. As a result they were often looked down on by the journeymen: 'They used to make them chargehand because they were no good on the tools. They could talk a lot but they couldn't do the job.' At the larger firms, where a foremen might have hundreds of men under him, he relied on his chargehands to allocate men to individual jobs and to supervise.

In the workshops

Other trades in ship repair were based largely or even solely in the workshops, rather than out on the ships. The oldest of these was the blacksmith, which had originally been the main metal trade in ship repair. Despite the rise of other trades, there was still a great deal of blacksmith's work on a ship before the Second World War. As George Conroy explains:

"Blacksmith's work on the ships mainly concerned anything to do with lifting gear, derricks or cranes. Any ship-side guard rails or ladders, hatch companion ways, hatch ladders, guard stancheons down the hatches, anything to do with safety and the factory act. And of course anchors and cables: when a ship went into dry dock, the first thing they'd do was lay them out in the dock. The surveyor would come along and inspect the anchors and cables and decide if any repairs wanted doing."

Back at the workshops there would be a department concerned solely with the testing of chains and cables to safe working loads, so that certificates of seaworthiness could be issued by a representative of Lloyds, the insurers. Insulation work was always a mainstay of the blacksmiths:

"We used to make all the fittings for refrigerated compartments on ships. All the fittings had to be forged. We used to make door hinges, door locks, lifting gear, anything to do with the metal part of the insulating, that's what kept us busy."

Blacksmiths made all their own tools, and: 'any other department wanted tools of any sort, they'd come to the smithy... For about eighteen months I did nothing else but tools.' This included, in the age of coal-burning ships, the repair of the eight-foot 'slices' and 'rakes' used by ships' firemen. Blacksmiths also did a range of work which was not strictly 'ship' repair: overhauling mooring buoys and other work for the dock board; and repairing lifting gear and cargo-handling equipment for stevedoring firms. Blacksmiths would do 'unofficial' work for dockers, repairing their hooks:

"We used to repair them quite often, the dockers would come into the works either with a broken hook or a hook that had strained and wanted reshaping, we used to have dockers in two or three times a week. Just slip in when the boss wasn't looking, because of course in those days dockers always carried a hook."

Most blacksmith's work was carried out in the smithy, but there were some 'outside men' who would strip down anything on a ship that needed repairing and send it back to the works. The variety of this work appealed to Bob Morrison:

"We never used to know where we were going unless we had a really big job aboard the ship. I could be in Gladstone tomorrow and on Friday I could be in Garston or Brunswick Dock or over in Birkenhead, that's the way I liked it, never the same and you were your own bosses ..."

George Conroy describes the smithy at A & R Brown and how the blacksmiths and their 'strikers' worked:

"The smithy itself was a building about 25 feet wide and about 50, 60 or so feet long. There were five fires, three down one side, two on the other side. They were open, with a canopy over the fire, and a communal chimney out through the roof for the smoke. At the side of each fire was a tank called a bosh filled with water, for when you wanted to cool your tools, or when you were doing a forging and you wanted to cool part of it. It was a soil floor, because when you put hot metal down or hot tools or whatever, concrete would crack.

When the blacksmith was working at his fire he wore a canvas apron and so did his mate, the striker. The blacksmith would work on the anvil shaping something with a tool and the striker would use the heavy hammer. If it was something heavier, and it had to be forged, in the centre of the shop was a five hundred weight steam hammer, and in a little alcove off the shop was the boiler which provided the steam for this hammer."

Blacksmiths' strikers had to learn to hit left-handed, to reduce the chance of hitting the smith on the hand. Generally the same two men worked together, and usually a blacksmith worked at the same fire, as they tended to specialise in certain kinds of work:

Blacksmiths' shop at Grayson Rollo's Birkenhead works, 1950. William Gerald 'Gerry' Chattle (blacksmiths' striker) is on the far right
Loaned by Mrs. Winifred Hartless

"A man who was used to working on heavy types of work usually wasn't very good on small work, tools and clips. One chap was an absolute wizzard on chains, no matter how big or heavy, whether they wanted repairing or just an odd link renewing. He could just weave them and they'd always be perfect. But if you gave him some brackets to make he'd get himself into a hopeless tangle, because he'd worked on chains for most of his life."

Technological changes from the Second World War tended to make such specialist skills of the smiths redundant, as George Conroy explains:

"After the war prefabrication started to come in, you started to shape things so far and then burn them into shape with the cutter. Or you'd get two pieces of metal near to the shape you wanted and electric weld them together. It became a kind of work you didn't need as much training for. If you made a mistake you could always cover it up, whereas before if you made a mistake you had to start again."

After the war the apprentices had to learn oxygen cutting and welding, but some of the older blacksmiths resisted the changes: 'they couldn't understand the economic facts of life, they had to use it or they had had it'. But George Conroy is full of admiration for these older men with their traditional methods, who were kept on by A & R Brown when they took over Lamport and Holt's workshop in 1935:

"For the few years after I came out of my time and throughout the war, the blacksmiths that were working in our shop were exceptionally good skilled craftsmen . . . Charlie Lowry and Frank Greene, Harold Hawthorne, Charlie Lamb, they were absolute wizzards, it was a joy to see them get a piece of metal and make something with it, weave it, get it under the steam hammer. They were like sculptors."

The steam hammer operators and strikers were highly skilled workers in their own right, even though they did not serve an apprenticeship. As Mrs. Winifred Hartless recalls of her father William Gerald 'Gerry' Chattle, a blacksmith's striker at Grayson Rollo's:

"Mr. Rollo used to come into the smithy and he would put his gold Albert watch on the anvil. My father's blow was that accurate, it was not even scratched. He used to demonstrate to parties of schoolboys too."

A large variety of the items fitted on a ship, from the propellor down to the doorknobs, would have to be cast in a foundry. In the old days a patternmaker had to make, in wood, a replica of the item to be cast in metal. It was then the moulder's jobs to fit sand around the wooden pattern. The sand had special cohesive properties so that when the wooden pattern was removed the sand retained the shape. Molten metal was then poured into the mould, and left to cool to form the shape of the object required. The patternmakers were a small but highly skilled trade, able to work on the most intricate carvings in wood. It was anything but a dull, repetitive job because even if a hundred castings of one particular item were required, the patternmaker would only have to make one.

The moulder's job was also a highly skilled one, having to understand the different qualities of metals and moulding sands. According to Ernie Parker:

"You became the artist, a sand artist. A sculptor might make the pattern, but its the moulder who makes the

Moulders pouring molten metal into a mould, C & H Crichton, 1958
Loaned by Joe Duffy

bronze statue in the end, he's got to make the casting."

Once cooled, the casting would be cleared up by a worker known as a fettler. Brass castings would then be past on to the brassfinishers, who would turn the casting into the finished product using lathes, and a variety of hand tools. Iron and steel castings would be passed on to the turners. There were other important, highly skilled trades in ship repair that specialised in working in one metal: tinsmiths, or sheet metal workers, and coppersmiths.

The replacement and repair of furnishings was also an important part of the ship repair industry. There would be work in the crew's quarters on all ships, but obviously the bulk of the work was on the numerous passenger liners that came into Liverpool for an overhaul. Some firms employed joiners to make furniture; others such as A & R Brown, bought the frames in, but employed french polishers and upholsterers to work on them in their own workshops. The upholsterers were responsible for not only the springing, stuffing and covering of seating but also for bedding, including making mattresses, the laying of carpets and lino, and curtains and any other drapery. Both men and women worked in upholstery, but with a clear division of responsibility between the sexes. On seating, the upholsterer would fasten the webbing, springs, canvas, stuffing and wadding onto the wooden frame, and then mark up the size of the top, covering material. The material would then be cut to shape by a male 'cutter'. The upholsteress would then sew the covers into shape on a machine. The covers would then be fitted and tacked onto the chair by the upholsterer, which was a very exacting job:

> "There was an art in putting the cover on ... There was one chap who was sloppy and the boss used to say 'the bluebottles will break their bloody legs walking along this chair', meaning there was lumps in it! He was very particular."

After the cover had been tacked, it was hand-sewn into place by the women workers. The women did all the sewing work, and thus were primarily responsible for curtains and loose covers. The men would size up and cut the carpets to shape, the women machine sew them together.

Both men and women in the trade saw their work as highly skilled, 'an art form in a way'. Partly this was because the work was so varied: 'There was always something different coming up', 'A

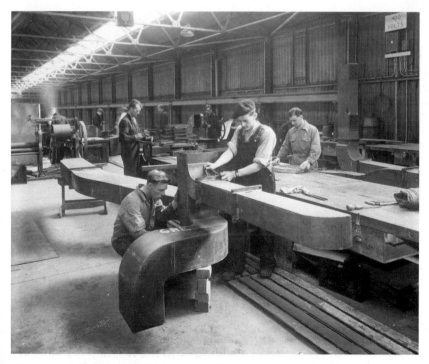

Sheet metal shop, C & H Crichton, 1950's
Source : Elsam, Mann & Cooper

typical day? There was no such thing'. If furniture was brought up to the workshops for repair, the laying of carpets and other work necessitated going onboard the ships. As Nelly Kenny recalls:

> "Sometimes they might get cigarette burns in a carpet or some damage, water damage, that piece would be cut out and we would have to go down and sew it in on our hands and knees... I didn't mind going down at all because it was a change, and it was quite an experience on the ships, its funny to see a ship when its undressed!"

Upholsterers on the roof of A & R Brown's upholstery workshops, Eleanor Street, Bootle, 1951. Back row, left to right: Edna Wall, Mary Tisdale, Margaret Kilbride, Nelly Bolshaw
Loaned by Mrs. Evelyn Douglas

The variety of work meant that there was a much more relaxed pattern of work, so that shipping upholstery work was preferable to other kinds. As William Kenny recalls:

> "In shipping you were never really chased. It was a different sort of thing to being in the retail or wholesale trade in a shop. You were stuck to times for jobs in those

shops, you could get 4 hours to do a settee, $4\frac{1}{2}$ to do a chair. But in shipping they really couldn't put times on jobs because everything was totally different each time, you'd never get two jobs alike."

There would also be a wide variety of office staff at each ship repair firm. John Thompson describes the main office at A & R Brown where he was a junior cost clerk in the late 1930's:

"The office was on the second floor facing the docks and the overhead railway. There were high desks right round the windows and right round the sides of the wall, and they had high stools. You could stand at the desk if necessary and move from one desk to another, so that you could gather information and work for quite a considerable period standing. There was a great iron safe in the office where the cash and books were kept and an ordinary open fire-place with a guard around it. And in the office there would be the chief clerk, Fred Heaton, assistant chief clerk Arthur Gatliffe, and the cashier Oliver Rathbone, secretary in an adjoining office, Mr. Lawson, the buyer, Harold Smith, an office boy, Kenneth Evans, and myself. And two more elderly clerks, one of whom used to a double key typewriter."

There were also draughtsmen to prepare detailed drawings of the repair work required. The managing director, Fred Warwick, 'had an office adjoining the cost office. He had an electric push button bell with codes. He would ring 1, 2, 3 or 4 and when you got your code number you'd go in and speak to him. He was brusque, what is known as a rough diamond. He'd worked hard I suppose as an engineer in his life out in the States.'

Brown's also had a time office in what was previously a pub on Boundary Street. First thing in the morning the timekeepers went down to ships to sign on the men; during the day they worked on the wages. All who worked at A & R Brown will remember Davy Adair: 'He never did anything else but give out tickets to the men who were going down on jobs, for the overhead or the tram. He was a character, there was no doubt about it. He used to stand on his dignity and if he thought he was getting a bit busy he'd slam his little shutter down and make them wait.'

44

GRAYSON, ROLLO & CLOVER DOCKS LTI

TELEGRAMS:
REGULATOR
LIVERPOOL

TELEPHONE
BOOTLE
1881

SHIP   REPAIRERS   ENGINEERS
DRYDOCK   OWNERS

4.   Conditions

The Working Environment

Working conditions out in the docks could be very poor, as every ship repairer will recall:

> "We used to dread the winter with a tug going in the dry dock, oh it was terrible. Outside on that staging and the wind blowing, whistling down the dock, and the dock dripping water, it was perishing. We used to tie old cement bags round our legs to keep warm!"

Some places were notoriously bad: 'the west corner of Gladstone, pneumonia corner we used to call it.' It could be almost as cold on board a ship: 'Working on ships on the docks in winter, believe me it was cold, because there was nothing but steel around you, and you couldn't move your fingers they were that cold.' Wet conditions could not interfere with work: 'You were there in hail, rain or snow, nobody ever knocked off work on account of the rain'; 'I've been up the mast in snow...I've drilled holes up there with the drilling machine in snow.' The only jobs that could be held up by rain were caulking or welding out on deck, but there would always be plenty of other work for shipwrights and welders to do.

Scaling was not the only dirty and unpleasant job on board the ships. Most trades were exposed to dirty conditions at some time, but found it much harder to get the 'dirt money' that scalers were entitled to. Of the trades based in the workshops, the moulders endured the worst conditions. Ernie Parker recalls working in a foundry in the 1940's:

"You were continually working on your knees. It was very dirty, very heavy, and if they were casting, very very hot. The sand became tremendously black with it being burnt, and also through adding coal dust and graphite to it. Your clothes would be black right through. Your old lady would have a hell of a job washing your underwear, everything was black. The showers didn't come till about 1946-47. You'd be worse than a coalman."

Washing facilities out on the docks at this time were equally primitive:

"If it was a long job you would keep a wooden box with your overalls in, and an old bucket and a bit of soap and a towel, so you could get a wash before you went home. You'd make a bit of a hut out of scrap wood and a bit of canvas, whatever you could find on the quay. The firm weren't interested at all in conditions. You were just sent to a ship to do the job. You had no facilities at all."

Toilet facilities were no better in the 1940's:

"We had the only air-conditioned toilets in Europe. There was one big pipe that went along with holes in the top of it and it went right to the river that, the wind blowing up from the river, you can imagine. And the lads used to do strange things, they'd get a piece of wood and put four nails in it and they'd put a tallow candle in, and float it with a stick. Imagine somebody sitting on a toilet with a lighted candle going past!"

Until the Second World War there were no canteens in the docks, so tea had to be made either on a brazier on the quayside or in the galley of a ship, using an enamel can or a six pound marmalade jar:

"You had a brew of tea, made up of tea, sugar, and condensed milk, and it was wrapped in a piece of the *Echo* or another newspaper. When you unwrapped it to put it in the boiling water, it was difficult to get the sticky part with the condensed milk off, so you used to put the whole thing in the water, print and everything. But the *Echo* tasted nice!"

Before the canteens lunchtime would be spent out on the quayside on a nice day, the top of the engine room or any other warm corner of the ship on a bad day; "the young ones would play football at the bottom of the graving docks, there was no danger of the ball going over the wall and getting lost! You'd play cards, 'solo' whist was the game".

Conditions in the workshops in the 1930's were just as primitive, and as out on the ships, there were no 'official' tea breaks:

"If the boss saw you making a can of tea, he'd just knock it over. If you wanted a cup of tea during the morning you just had to keep it out of his sight . . . and he had an eagle eye!"

Welders from Grayson Rollo, who were working on the *Palomares*, January 1947. Behind them on the quayside is the makeshift tea-hut they built themselves out of scrap from the ship
Loaned by John 'Jack' Waggott who is fourth from the left on the back row

In the 1940's cafes sprang up around the works, but these are not always fondly remembered. As Ted Seddon recalls of A & R Brown,

"There was a little canteen, cocoa rooms, outside, and you used to call it Ma Brown's. You used to go down four or five steps, just like a little kitchen. She used to have a stocking with the tea in hanging in the urn!"

It was no great loss when Brown's took it over and turned it into an armature shop!

Casualism

The wages of ship repairers were always nominally as good as those of workers in similar jobs in the general engineering industry. However, until the 1960's, ship repairers were employed on a casual basis, in a similar way to the dockers. They were never guaranteed a full working week because there was always a varying demand for labour in the industry. Men were needed when a ship came in, and could be laid off as soon as the repairs were completed. The demand for ship repairers, therefore, varied on a day-to-day basis, depending on how many ships were in port and required repairs. It also varied with the seasons, as George Conroy explains:

"From October to about March was a busy time, because it was a quiet time for the passenger liners. They all used to come into port and have an annual overhaul, all the Cunarders, the White Star Liners, Canadian Pacific vessels, which meant a lot of employment. Summer was always a slack time on the ship repairing side, mainly general maintenance".

Those who worked mainly on the liners found their work the most seasonal. As John Rock remembers,

"In upholstery you worked for about six months of the year on ships. They would start to liven up roundabout October and go right through till the following May. Then from May until the October you worked in the town shops where you get on for a short time. They were busy in the summer, and then you went back to the shipping. The shipping people got by far the best money, some of the town were more permanent".

On the other hand, Dave Langton recalls that at Cubbin's the summer months were busiest, working on the annual overhauls of Rea's tugs. During the slack season unemployed ship repairers would look for jobs in the general engineering industry, particularly, in later years, in car factories. Some, such as plumbers, could hope to find work in the building industry.

All ship repairers recall their complete lack of job security until redundancy legislation came into effect in 1965. Before then,

"You were casual labour, you could be stopped at an hour's notice. You worked every hour you were there, if there was no work you were laid off. They could come to you at four o'clock in the afternoon and say 'don't come in the morning'."

Ship repairers could be taken on for just one day or even half a day. However, some were much more regularly employed than others. Skilled apprenticed tradesmen were much more likely to get regular work than scalers and labourers. Their skills were often in short supply. Those who were based in the workshops were much more likely to get regular work than those who worked on the ships: "As soon as that ship went out and there was nothing coming in, they'd be fired". But in the workshops it was always likely that there would be something for the men to do even when there were no ships under repair by the firm. By the same token the degree of casualism varied from trade to trade. Patternmakers and brassfinishers, based in the workshops, could be constantly employed; at the other extreme 'docking' shipwrights had no guarantee of work from day-to-day. There were also variations from firm to firm. 'Half-day Jack' at Grayson's south shop was notorious for laying men off as soon as possible; Campbell and Isherwood, on the other hand, were a firm that had a good reputation for keeping men on standby, paying them standard wages. Within each trade some workers would be preferred at a particular firm to others. It was all a question of becoming a 'regular', being 'known'. How was this done? Perhaps you had served your apprenticeship at a firm and were known as a good worker. Equally, it might depend on having a relative at a firm; or simply whether or not your 'face' fitted with the foreman.

For all these reasons, some men were almost constantly employed year after year by the same firm, while others had to move from firm to firm, picking up a day's work here and there. Ted Seddon, a brassfinisher, is an example of the former:

"You were only a casual worker. Even though I was in the shipping game for 41 years, I was still classed as a casual worker after all those years ... But I think I was only laid off about three times in the 41 years I was at A & R Brown. Twice for a week or so I'd be off and then they'd send for me, and then there was one time I was off for about six weeks, then they sent for me".

On the other hand, Tom Fairbrother recalls that in his twelve years as a scaler,

"the longest job I ever got was four weeks. You're hired, jobs done, you're fired, there was no such thing as a week in hand or anything like that. You just walked into a pub on the dock road and kept your ears open, 'I believe so and so's hiring'."

The experience of most ship repairers lay somewhere in between the almost constant employment at one firm of Ted on the one hand and Tom's almost daily search for work on the other.

Before the war nearly all ship repair workers, skilled and unskilled, were taken on, like dockers, at 'stands'. There were fifty or so recognised stands in the area, whether by a firm's workshops or by the graving docks. Word would get around when work was coming up, as George Conroy explains:

"If you were going to get busy there'd be men waiting at the door. The grapevine, they'd get to know. The word would go round that A & R Brown has got a ship starting and they want boilermakers, blacksmiths, painters, plumbers, fitters, and you'd see a crowd of men".

But it was not a lottery as to who was taken on:

"We used to line up on the wall. The man who was well known, it didn't matter whether he stood at the back or the front, he knew very well he was on. But those who weren't as well known wanted to be in the front so the boss could see them".

As Ken Patterson recalls of A & R Brown:

"When I started they used to have them lined up on the dock road. The boss used to go to the upstairs window and say 'we'll have that one and that one, not that one he's a troublemaker'. The chargehand used to go out and say 'you, you and you, start, the rest away'."

One way to get work ahead of others was to offer a bribe to a foreman, whether a drink, or money passed over in a box of matches. This was said to be rife in the depression of the 1930's when men were desperate for work. It seems to have continued among the scalers and other unskilled labour after the war. Tom Fairbrother recalls that on the stand for scalers at A & R Brown just after the war, several men gave the foreman half a crown when they were chosen. It seemed to be done by 'men who were getting on in years', and who therefore might be getting too old for heavy manual labour. But in the skilled trades, old age does not seem to have been a handicap. Edward Bowyer worked as a shipwright in his seventies! And this was not uncommon.

The stand system was degrading, often corrupt, and also very inefficient as a means of allocating labour. During the Second World War, the Government introduced a more formal system to organise the hiring of the skilled tradesmen, which was less open to abuse. As a foreman explains,

" 'B' Clearing House was a labour exchange on the dock road. All the ship repair men from both sides of the river were registered there as being employed or unemployed. If I wanted a man, I knew who I'd want, I would ring up the clearing house about 4 o'clock in the afternoon. They

Cecil Roberts (left), Leonard Miles (right), upholsterers at A & R Brown, in the docks where they were working on board a ship, late 1940's
Loaned by John Rock

would send him a telegram saying report to Sandhills in the morning, and my man would be there without fail".

It would be wrong to give the impression that the casual system was entirely bad for the workers. In the post-war period, when there was plenty of work, and at times a shortage of skilled labour, tradesmen could exert some choice over which firm they worked for. They could often leave one job and step into another straight away. The casual system meant that a worker could equally give his *employer* only one hours' notice. One might choose to go for a guaranteed longer engagement somewhere else: "A lot of men used to 'follow the money', they'd have maybe two days in Brown's and then they'd leave and go to Harland's, because there might be a six week job at Harland's". One might choose to move to a job with more overtime, or simply for a change of scene. Arthur Robinson:

"If we were going slack and there was no overtime in one place, and there was some work somewhere else, I'd go along and see if I could get a start. I would go back, get my cards that night, and start at the other place the next morning, because it was all casual work. They could sack you like that and you could do the same. I never liked being in a job too long, I used to get fed up. But I was never out of work".

It was possible to play the system against the firms:

"I hated Laird's, and I'd come out of Laird's after the war and started at Harland's and I didn't really want to go back. But it was the Easter holidays, and you got paid Easter Monday and Good Friday at Laird's. I went with another coppersmith named Bernie O'Neill. We went over and worked together as mates, we worked the Tuesday, the Wednesday and the Thursday and we were off Good Friday and Easter Monday. When we came in on the Tuesday we gave our notice in because we didn't like it! My mate Bernie, he went to Crichton's and I went to Coventry, but I got two days out of them for nothing. I deserved that for what they had done to me in the past!"

Nevertheless, the casual system of employment meant that many ship repairers would often fail to take home a 'full' week's wages. Most experienced odd days or weeks of unemployment at some time, even in the boom period of the industry in the 1940s and 1950s.

Overtime

Given the shipowners' need to get ships out in a hurry, overtime was a regular feature of ship repair. All-night working was not uncommon. While working an 'all night' was usually optional, it could be a mistake to turn it down: "If you didn't do it you weren't very popular. When it came to another time and you needed it, you wouldn't get the chance". Though the money might be useful 'all nights' were unpopular with many:

"It was always the curse of ship repair work, overtime. You never knew when you were getting home. When I was foreman at Crichton's it got worse than ever because I used to get called out at all hours of the day and night. They put a phone in for me, it was nothing for me to get a phone call at 11 or 12 o'clock at night. I didn't have a car, I used to have a private phone number to get a taxi and take me down to a ship and get men out, that was a common occurrence".

'Allnights' were particularly unpopular with foremen, who often did not get paid for overtime. Apprentices could find all-night working a strain—and Leslie I'Anson recalls that it was compulsory:

"The foreman would come to you at 2 minutes to 5 and say "you, you and you get back here at 7 o'clock, you're working all night". "Mr. Clarkson, I'm going to nightschool tonight". "Not tonight your not, your working for us, be back here for 7 o'clock". You didn't argue with him. You'd go home, have your dinner, get fresh sandwiches, a fresh brew of tea, one for your supper and one for your breakfast, and then you'd go back. At 7 o'clock you'd go down to the Langton Dock, the graving dock where the ship was lying. It would probably be a job where you would have to take the propeller off, which could weigh anything up to twenty tons. You'd work from 7 o'clock till midnight and then you'd go for your supper which was 12 till half past 12. Then you'd work through until 7 o'clock the following morning and then go for your breakfast. I was telling a young fella this once and he said to me "ah, then you'd go home". I said "Oh no you didn't, you started a fresh day's work!"

It was only from the 1950's that workers were given the next day off with pay. Tom Hartley remembers a 72-hour stint!: "When I did get off I slept about 3 days and nights. What a game that was ... I don't know how you get used to it, we were like walking ghosts!".

On the other hand, one could get lucky, and be paid for the night without having to work it all. Once 11.30 p.m. was passed, the full night's overtime had to paid: "You got some soft ones where perhaps you'd be away about two o'clock in the morning—just luck of the draw". Or perhaps "about one o'clock in the morning, the chargehands would say 'right lads, you've done enough', so you just got down in any quiet corner you could. Next day of course you were expected to work all day". Alternatively the men might choose to forego their supper break from 9 p.m. to 11 p.m. and work right through, so they could be away for the last bus or tram, and still have done enough hours for an 'all-night'.

In the Second World War, ship repairers had to work exceptionally long hours. Many recall regular overtime till 9 o'clock at night, after a 7.30 a.m. start, and Sunday working was quite common. There was also the uncertainty of never knowing when a shift of overtime might finish, as for security reasons no one would be told how much repairs there were to do on a ship, or when it was to sail. Mrs. Hartley recalls the effects on family life:

"He might manage to get home at five and he'd just rush in and say 'pack up enough sandwiches for all tonight and all tomorrow, we've got a rush job on'. He didn't even stop for tea or anything, I'd be cutting sandwiches like crazy, and he'd rush off again saying 'expect me when you see me'. He'd be out all night and all the next day and one time he was out all the next night as well. He came home in the middle of the day afterwards, sat down, lit his pipe, set himself on fire and went fast asleep...Wouldn't have needed an incendiary bomb would we?! I had to keep introducing the children to him, "this is your father", and they'd just say 'oh'".

Long hours at work might be followed by a couple of hours of duty each night and one entire night per week as an ARP warden or in the Home Guard.

Merseyside's ship repairers made a tremendous contribution to the war effort, some losing their lives in the process. In the opinion of many, that contribution has never been adequately acknolwedged. As one ship repairer recalls:

"Most of the good work was done on a Saturday in England during the war. At 12 o'clock all the officials seemed to vanish, and there was more work done on a Saturday afternoon and a Sunday by doing things in the way we'd always done them. It wasn't officialdom that won the war, it was the people. The people won the war by putting that extra bit in."

Perks

Ship repairers enjoyed some perks, not least hospitality from ship's officers when working overtime. There was also the chance of getting some duty free goods, as a fitter recalls:

"The ships engineer would say 'Do you smoke'? 'Yes! Yes!' 'Do you want 200 cigarettes, Camel or Lucky Strike, give us twelve bob and you can have a packet of them!' You were made up! You'd come back and flog them at 2 shillings a packet".

There were sometimes perks for upholsterers on board a ship. John Rock recalls stripping down seating on a large passenger liner:

"It was full of money all down the sides. I got the job of stripping it out and I could strip better than most. The faster I stripped it out the more money I got! Not a lot, four or five pounds maybe, but it was a lot in those days".

Shipwrights traditionally enjoyed one perk which had its origins in the 18th century, as Edward Bowyer recollects:

"When I first started in 1914 shipwrights took all the wood home that was chopped off. What falls from the axe belongs to the man, he can sell it, give it away or anything else. But after the war started, all that fell away and things got tighter and tighter. You can't take a bobbin home now".

But a tradition of being allowed to use scrap wood did continue: "they never stopped you making any little stools or anything like that, to take home". A welder recalls that making toys from scraps of metal and wood was a traditional perk in the forties and fifties: "Six weeks before Christmas, you'd see men busy in the corners making something. They'd make it in sections so they could get it past the policemen!"

With so many men in different trades and from different firms working out on a ship, it was hard for foremen to keep track of them all, and there were opportunities to 'sag off', or as the dockers termed it, go on the 'welt'. Welders worked in pairs, taking it in turns to weld. As one foreman recalls of the 1950's, the second man was supposed to act as 'safety' for the first, but "I would have a snap roll-call now and again, and it was amazing the number of fellas that didn't show up. They were either at home decorating or working for another firm! Whether they were keeping the chargehands

Son of a ship repairer with the toy aeroplane his father made from scrap in the workshops, about 1945

sweet or not I don't know". There were other perks which were tantamount to thieving. As one man recalls,

> "during the war we used to work on these frigates and the ratings would sell you a pair of officer's shoes. You could tell the officer's shoes, they were leather-lined, four shillings brand new, great!... I don't know where they got the shoes from, the officers must have been going bare-footed, the amount of pairs they used to sell".

Petrol from welding generators on the quay would sometimes be syphoned off overnight, and electric cable would go missing. However, even if thieving of materials was widespread, it seems clear that the bosses were able to work much bigger 'fiddles'. As a shipwright who began work in 1914 argues,

> "There's been thieving of materials ever since the world was built, from the shipowners down to the working man. That's why sometimes the bosses knew the working man was doing it but they couldn't do anything

because they were doing it themselves, only they were doing it with stuff of more value. The workman was only stealing shillings, they were stealing pounds, booking times for dead men. All ship repairers and ship builders had men on their list. They'd have 150 men listed working on that ship and there's not 50. For every man who goes to work the firm gets a fixed price for him. But if he goes aboard the ship, up the gangway and down the other one he's not there is he? But the firm still get their money. All firms did it".

Bosses and Unions

The working atmosphere and relations between bosses and workers varied from firm to firm, but seem to have been better at the smaller firms. Few ship repairers have a good word to say about Cammell Laird; whereas those who worked at A & R Brown recall a relaxed and friendly atmosphere. The management were much

Managers and foremen from Grayson Rollo's, 1950's, including Ted Rogers, Sid Mooney, George Allen, George Taylor, Johnny Watts
Loaned by John Waggott

more approachable at the smaller firms. Tom Hartley recalls of Crichton's that "If anything was wrong they'd listen to you. You could have a row and go straight to the managing director, Pike, hell of a nice fellow". Dave Langton remembers of working at Cubbin's in the fifties that "Bert Cubbin would take his coat off and roll his sleeves up, though he was the boss, his name was on the gate".

None of the firms, however, offered much in the way of fringe benefits to their workers. From the 1940's some firms, like A & R Brown, gave office staff and foremen help with mortgages, and ran pension schemes, but they offered nothing to the shopfloor workers. Even though ship repairs were officially employed on a casual basis until the 1960's, some worked for the same firm all their working lives. Yet these workers received no recognition when it came to retirement. Mrs. Winifred Hartless recalls how her father, William Gerald (Gerry) Chattle, came to retire from Grayson's after 50 years with the firm:

> "My father was so sad, when, at the age of 72 years, my mother told him to finish work, as with his wage, plus their pensions, he was being too heavily taxed. So I wrote a letter on his behalf to the management, saying he thought it time to finish his service. He never ever received a reply, it really broke his heart. So shortly after his death, I went to Grayson Rollo to express my disgust at the way my dear father was so shabbily treated after 50 years of devoted service. He never got so much as a token for when he retired or even a flower when he died. He was a fine man, a dedicated employee, but sad to say not appreciated by the employers of a bygone era".

Nevertheless, the casual system of employment meant that many ship repairers would often fail to take home a 'full' week's wages.

Merseyside's ship repairers first saw the need to combine to protect their interests in the 1790's, when the Liverpool shipwrights' union was founded. There has been a strong tradition of trade unionism in the industry ever since. William Kenny argues why trade unionism was vital for the upholsterers in the 1930's:

> "If you were in a union shop you had to be in the union, but it did give you a certain amount of security as regards your wages. The unions came to an arrangement that they pay £2 15s a week. You could go to a non-union ship and you might only be working for £2 a week. Other shops, piece work used to be the game, you'd get so much per item, so much for a settee, so much for a chair. They used to be real sweat shops".

However, during the mass unemployment of the 1920's and 1930's the unions were comparatively weak. Only the smaller trades like coppersmiths and patternmakers were able to enforce a 'closed shop', i.e. you had to be a member of the union to work at the trade. The Second World War strengthened the unions' position, but in George Connoy's view, it was "In the 1950's that the unions began to take a stronger line. Eventually, if you were not in the union you couldn't be taken on. When I had to start men, a man had to produce his union card and he had to be in a certain union".

Once source of weakness for the unions in ship repair was that there were so many of them: initially at least, one for each trade. It was only in 1963 that the boilermakers, shipwrights and blacksmiths became united in a single union; later moves brought many of the engineering trades together in the AUEW. The large number of unions weakened their collective hand in disputes with the employers, though there was the Confederation of Shipbuilding and Engineering Unions which aimed to bring the unions together. A further problem caused by having a union for each trade were the large number of demarcation disputes between the unions: should a particular job be carried out by members of their trade or by a member of another? Changes in technology, ship design, and machinery only served to make the distinctions between the trades even more complex. Arthur Robinson recalls that his trade, the coppersmiths, and the plumbers were 'always at one another's throats'. Each trade had detailed demarcation books (often running into 80 to 90 pages) to refer to, because the distinction as to whose work was whose could be very minor:

"The dividing line was so thin. A clip on a pipe would go to the blacksmiths up to a certain thickness. If you only wanted light clips for light pipes it would go to the sheet metal workers. If it was a fabricated one it would go to the boilermakers. Only a clip, but by defining what it was made of you found which trade it went to".

While it would be wrong to over-exaggerate the role of such disputes, they could only weaken the trade union movement. They gave employers an opportunity to play up divisions between the unions. Firms used demarcation disputes to attempt to erode the power of the unions, and impose harsher working practices.

If relations between the unions of different trades were sometimes strained, relations between workers in different trades on the shop floor or on the ships were usually good-natured. As Tom Hartley remembers of A & R Brown, "Brown's shop, as old as it was, was a happy shop, there was never any backbiting, a good crowd . . . Say you want something making for home, you'd just say which department will make me one of those? It would be done". On pay day at Brown's a collection was always made for those off sick. Tempers, of course, did sometimes flare up on a job. Tom Hartley recalls a 'run-in' with a scaler, who he fended off with an electric shock!: "One big fella, he was going to kill me on one ship. So I put my fingers on one of the electrical boards right by, and the other hand on his face—he was screaming to death! I could stand most currents of electrics. So every time that he used to come near me I'd stick a little bit of wire out of my pocket and wave it at him, and he was off!"

One factor which in earlier days may have caused divisions among ship repairers, even within the some trade, was religion. However, few remember differences between Catholics and Protestants as being of any significance at work from the 1920s onwards. In the opinion of Edward Bowyer, shipwright:

"Religion never came into the question. There was Catholics and Protestants and Welshmen and Scotsmen. There was no mention of it, unless it was in a joking way. There was two lads named Davy: Catholic Davy and Protestant Davy, and that's all there was to it, 'Where's Protestant Davy?' 'Oh he's with so and so'. That's the only way you got it. Oh no, there was no religion in the business".

However, in the mid 1950's the Catholic church was still able to exert some influence in the workplace. Local priests launched a campaign encouraging Catholic trade unionists in the industry to stand as shop stewards, to oppose a supposed 'communist' takeover of the unions.

There is a popular image of the unions in shipbuilding (and by inference in ship repair) enjoying great power and being strike prone. Yet major strikes in both of these industries on Merseyside have been relatively few and far between. In the opinion of one foreman in the industry from the 1940's to the 1960's,

"I'm amazed that the men weren't militant, and lets face it, they had every reason to be. Its degrading for a man to be suddenly told at half past four that he's finishing tonight at half past five".

In the inter-war period mass unemployment put trade unionists in too weak a position to mount an effective strike in the industry:

"In those days the situation was that they could pick somebody up for your job just like that. There were men with qualifications standing outside. So if you had a dispute, there was the door, there was another man there who could do you job equally well".

Even after the war strikes at many firms were few and far between. Amy Beattie worked at Rutherford's in Birkenhead from 1943 to 1961, and recalls only one strike in that time, which lasted three weeks. The one major dispute that all ship repairers will remember was in the summer of 1961. The boilermakers struck for an extra pound a week, and most of the other trades soon joined in. The boilermakers were successful after 13 weeks; other trades were out for 16 weeks in total, before they secured the same rise. One man recalls the financial hardships of the strike:

"We were staying with the wife's mother and her name was on the rent book so we didn't get any money. All I got from Social Security was a few shillings for the baby. It was hard going, I had to use all the savings I had got with my overtime. We were back to square one then".

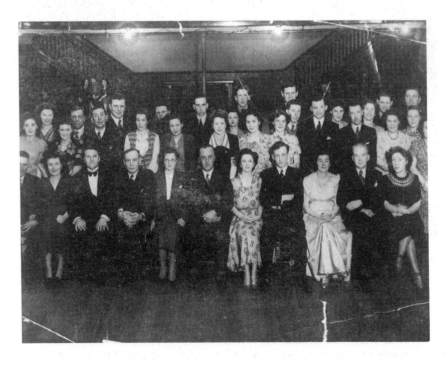

A & R Brown social at the Cafe Nord, North John Street, Liverpool, probably 1943
Loaned by John Antrobus

Leisure

One way for the firms to maintain good relations with their workers was to provide leisure facilities. Harland and Wolff had a large Recreation Association which ran sporting events and teams of all kinds, and a social club. But this was not to everyone's liking: "I went once or twice but I didn't fancy it. I don't believe in mixing with the bosses anyway". Firms such as Grayson's and Crichton's, however, never took the trouble. In the 1920's, when John Larking ran A & R Brown, he organised coach trips to Blackpool. Brown's

A & R Brown works' outing, 1950's. Back row left to right: Nobby Clarke, W. Clare, Ken Patterson, ?, Ted Lee, Roy Finlay, Alec Oldfield, ? Lawson. Front row, left to right: Jack Gilgrass, Ron Thornton, Ted Seddon
Loaned by Ted Seddon

management held a few socials during the war, but one at the Cafe Nord in North John Street in 1943 was the last—and perhaps the reason why they never bothered again is clear:

"It was one of those where there's a dance on and a buffet, and the bosses tried to mingle with the staff. I don't know that they succeeded very well because most of the men were at the bar! And us ladies were sitting there like wallflowers trying to get a dance out of somebody . . . You could take visitors but you had to pay a nominal amount for their tickets. This friend we took was so fed up with all these stuck up ninny's that were with the bosses, that she grabbed a handful of sandwiches and rammed them in the pockets of their fur coats!"

Brown's had a very active social club after the war but it was run by the men themselves. Though there were no social club premises, rooms were hired for dances, socials and dinners. There was also an annual outing of three or four coachloads, as Ted Seddon recalls:

"They used to take you out, maybe to Buxton for your dinner, and from there you'd go to Matlock. On the way home we'd go to a pub and there'd be tea laid out, and then they'd have a band, a paid artist to entertain us, there was dancing, oh they were great!"

The social club also ran a popular and successful football team which played in the Liverpool Business House League. The club colours were maroon and yellow, which matched the livery of the firm's four wagons. The inspiration behind the team was Sid Rudd, who has since become a leading figure in the Football Association. Mike Smith, an apprentice brassfinisher at Brown's in the fifties, recalls the football team with affection:

"Our two most loyal supporters were Davy Adair and Fred Mears. They never missed a match. Fred was the trainer, Davy would run the line, in trilby and gaberdine mackintosh. Occasionally, if he'd had a drop of Guinness beforehand he would wander slowly in-field, ending up near the penalty area, handkerchief waving away. Jack Simpson, Brown's first-aid man, and Ted Lee of the brass-shop also supported us. Ken Patterson, the skipper, played centre half, he wasn't very tall but he was so strong in the tackle. Veteran Bert Hanson, a 'tinwacker' from the famous Aintree footballing family, played left back after a career with Marine. Other regular players were John 'Taffy' Brown, Georgie Garner and George Ashworth, outside blacksmiths, Barny Reilly, a tinwacker, and Tommy Newcombe. The other positions were usually filled by apprentices. Peter Hughes, Tommy Caldwell, Jim 'Bomber' Cockburn, Harry Price, Don Hunter, Brian Duffy, George Cribb, Jock the tinsmith, Johnny Warner, Dick Graham, Jerry Kehoe, Davy Mears, John Church, Ronnie Ashton (brother of Billy J. Kramer) and 'Yogi' the plumber all played for Brown's at some stage. Apprentices who weren't so keen on football were John

Inman, Jimmy Formby, Tommy Forsythe, Dougie Johnson, Brian Roberts, Luke Walsh, Alan Bell, Charlie Drought, Norman Poppett, Ginger Hughes, Geoff Appleton, Eddie Taylor, Les Jones, Phillip Mears, Maurice Entwistle, John Hoey, and many more to whom I beg forgiveness for forgetting their names".

A & R Brown's football team, 1945-6 : League champions, second division, Liverpool Business House League, and also cup finalists.
Back row, left to right: A. Galcliffe, Fred Mears, Tommy Watts, J. Dickson, B. Smy, ? Dickson, Mr. Graham.
Middle row, left to right: Sid Rudd, Peter Hodgson, Tom Gribben, Frank Plunkett, Charlie Hope, ? Cahill, Billy Scott, Jack Arnold, Ted Lee.
Front row, left to right: Fred Warwick, Jackie Cotterill, Gordon White, Tom Bulmer, George Stein, Billy Prior, Fred Galeteley, Alan Craig, Victor Mangham.
Loaned by John and Joyce Thompson

Brown's veterans will also recall that Alec Oldfield attended every match, and drew a cartoon of the game which was duly pinned up on the notice board every week.

Even when the industry was in its heyday, the working lives and conditions of ship repairers were always tough. There was the constant threat of dismissal at an hour's notice, and no reward for long and faithful service to any firm. It was only their trade unionism, and their mutual aid and camaraderie, both at work and in their leisure time, that enabled ship repairers to make their own working lives tolerable.

LIVERPOOL:
TELEPHONES: BOOTLE 2493-2494.
AFTER HOURS: CROSBY 510.
GREAT CROSBY 4510
TELEGRAMS "ISOLA" LIVERPOOL.

REGISTERED

BRISTOL CHANNEL:
TELEPHONES: NEWPORT, MON. 3792.
TELEGRAMS "ISOLA" NEWPORT, MON.
GLASGOW:
TELEPHONE: " SOUTH 2343.
TELEGRAMS "INSULATION" GLASGOW.

THE MERSEY INSULATION COMPANY, LTD.

SHIP REPAIRERS, JOINERS, CARPENTERS, PAINTERS & DECORATORS.

5. Hazards

Shipbuilding has been one of the more dangerous industries to work in—and ship repair appears to have been equally hazardous! Dave Langton recalls the dangers of working in a ship's engine room in the 1950's:

> "You're in an engine room, and she's getting side plates done, and there's a compressor getting lifted up and over your head. They're burning the plate off over there, and all of a sudden the burners start sparking all over you, no one shouts 'look out'...If someone shouted 'look out below' your eyes were everywhere, something was falling. There were no safety helmets then".

As common as being hit by falling material was to fall oneself. Tripping and falling down the hatches of ships is remembered as a 'regular event' and most ship repairers can remember a fatal incident. Just as common was falling off the side of a ship, perhaps from staging, into the dry dock. Edward Bowyer, shipwright recalls:

> "You never know when there's going to be an accident on board a ship, knocked off a stage, fall off a stage. I only fell off one, that was in dry dock. I just forgot myself on the stage, stood back to look at it and went over. It was only about fiteen feet, only a little cut on me head, nothing much. Just imagine, how you fall and what you fall on".

But more serious accidents of this kind are remembered by many ship repairers. George Conroy:

"When painters were working over the side on the ships they just used to stand on a little plank about 10 or 12 inches wide, 9 or 10 feet long, and it was just suspended by a single rope. I remember a fella doing that and the rope

C & H Crichton employees working on the *Leviathan* in Gladstone graving dock, 1960
Loaned by Jack McAllister

carried away and he went right in the dock. He didn't survive".

The following is from the records of accidents of dock board employees:

Report of August 8, 1929 from the Engineer with regard to an accident which John Higgins, Riveter in his Department, met with on board, No. 36. Steam Hopper Barge in the Herculaneum Graving Dock No. 3, on that date:

Higgins was standing on a staging unscrewing a bolt on the vessel's draw bar when the spanner he was using slipped off the head of the bolt causing him to overbalance and fall a distance of about 10 feet on to the bottom of the Graving Dock, severely injuring his head.

Higgins died as a result of his injury on the 10th of August.

There was also the danger of falling from a ship's mast for riggers, and for electricians like Tom Hartley who would have to go up to repair mast headlights. And as he recalls, though there was danger money for this, it was just "half a crown a day. You'd be up there from seven o'clock in the morning till seven o'clock at night, and it would still only be a half a crown".

Steam was another source of danger on a ship, as Leslie I'Anson remembers:

"One of my friends, Percy Dunning, was working on some valves on the boiler face, and while he was doing this one of the engineers of the ship came down to the engine room. He was drunk and he turned on the intermediate stock valve between a live boiler and and boiler that Percy was working on. The steam came up through the blow-down valve and scalded this friend of mine. When they took his overalls off they took all his skin off as well. He was in terrible agony".

This story at least had a happy ending: he married the nurse who looked after him in Bootle General Hospital! But fatal accidents of this kind were not uncommon. As John Thompson recalls:

"On one occasion there were a number of scalers inside a boiler, cleaning and scraping and scaling away, when accidentally somebody turned a valve. The steam ran from one boiler into the other, and they were killed of course".

There were other possible causes of fatalities: fire; electrocution; and explosions or suffocation caused by the build-up of gases in tanks. A chemist would always have to check that a ship was free from dangerous gases before work could begin. Welders faced the hazard of burns:

"You always had holes in your shirts from sparks and now and again your overalls would start smouldering. You'd have a hole there when you noticed it. There was a smell and you knew it was your overalls, so you just squeezed it. Welding overhead, something would go down your sleeve or your chest, if you had an open neck shirt. You got these burns, and you learnt yourself that you must let them die out themselves, you mustn't try to put them out because you're pushing the burn further in."

Welders also faced the problem of flashes:

"If you just couldn't get the arc to strike you might take your screen away for a minute to see where you were. The electrode would touch the metal and you got a flash. Mostly the men working with the welders, they would get the flashes, they'd get a flash bouncing off a white bulkhead, hitting their eyes . . . It made you feel as though you've got sand in your eyes . . . Some of the welders used to go off sick with a flash, some are more prone than others, I seemed to weather them better than some people. It wasn't classed as an industrial injury so they just got basic sick pay, an industrial injury you got more pay. Eventually it was made an industrial injury".

If working out on the ships in the graving docks was the most dangerous part of ship repair, many of those I spoke to recalled fatal accidents in the workshops. Less serious accidents were just as common, and not just minor cuts and bruises. For patternmakers, the more cutting machinery there was, the greater the dangers, which, as Ken Patterson recalls, made the more antiquated department at A & R Brown safer:

"You used to see a lot of the patternmakers from the other firms, bigger machine shop firms, Harland's and Rollo's, they'd have tips of fingers missing. Not with carelessness or anything. I was lucky with just a few stitches here and a few stitches there. You got little nicks and that. I don't think it was any more dangerous than any other department".

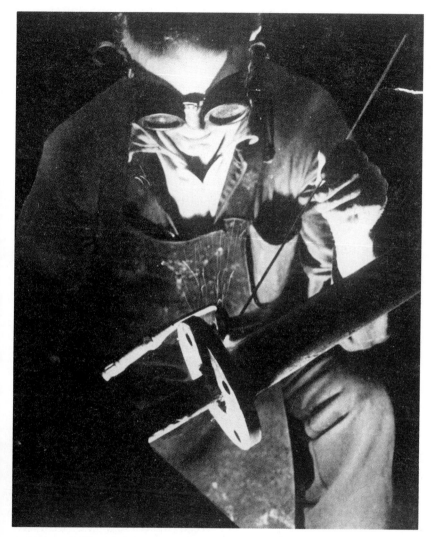

Welder at work, C & H Crichton promotional calendar, 1958
Loaned by Joe Duffy

For blacksmiths, the perennial problem was burns. Amy Beattie
remembers several accidents:

> "One day I got a bit of steel in my hand and tried poultices
> to get it out. I couldn't get it out and I had to go to hospital
> for them to open it. Another time I got hold of a black hot

bar and it stuck to my hand, oh god. I went to the hospital and they cut all the blisters, I had a terrible hand, fortunately it was the left one. I'd been helping, holding up, and I didn't know he'd turned the bar round in the fire and I'd put my hand on it to hold it. Another time a hot bar swung round and went right across my back, burnt a hole in my boiler suit, right through to the skin".

But each time after going to hospital, she was back at work the next day: "You didn't stay off work then. Your head would have to be hanging off before you stayed off!"

The most dangerous kind of work away from the ships was that of the moulders. Ernie Parker:

"I never had an accident, I was pretty lucky in my working life, not that I was any more extra careful than anybody else. The odd burn, you could be working away and something could blow up over there and fly over and burn you. I got burnt on the back of my neck once and it turned septic. They were casting and it blew up. It flew through the air and went down my neck, I was kneeling down doing my job.

The pressure is tremendous, imagine all the gas that is building up off the metal, and its got to get out somewhere. If you haven't got the right vents so it can escape it will just burst out, it will find the weakest spot. One foundry I worked in in Speke, something similar to that happened and it blew the bar of a box out, and there was about six badly burned, but the chap that was right by it got the lot."

In the 1930's first aid provision was very primitive, as Leslie I'Anson recalls of Crichton's:

"All that you had was a first aid box in the stores. There'd be a bottle of iodine and a bandage and some cotton wool and that was probably the extent of it in those days. They just cleaned it up and put iodine on it and bound you up."

Things were only marginally better at Grayson's in the 1940's:

"On a small ship you usually went to one of the crew, maybe the chief officer had a first aid box, or there was usually somewhere on the dock estate where there was a first aid man. But on a large ship they had a first aid man on the ship. At Grayson Rollo's the first aid man for the whole of the works was in the main gatehouse, that was it. So it was really basic, anything serious you were sent up to one of the hospitals."

Government regulations were introduced in the 1960's to the effect that if there were more than eight men working on a ship, there had to be a first-aid man present. Sometimes the box keeper, who stored the tools in the dry dock, would double as first-aid man. There also had to be a first-aid room and staff at the workshops. Being a first-aid attendant out on the ships was an attractive job, as: "they were dressed in a suit, not in a pair of overalls. They got all the overtime going because they automatically worked what the men worked." On the other hand, they suffered from the effects of casualism as badly as the others out on the ships:

> "You could have 20 ships working and you'd have 20 first-aid men on them. But they used to get laid off like the boilermakers. Twenty ships today, if there was only 10 tomorrow they didn't keep the 10 first aiders on, they used to sack them. They'd go along the road to Rollo's."

Ship repairers faced greater dangers at work during the war, as safety measures were often ignored in the rush to get ships out:

The *Ascanius* in dry dock at Cammell Laird after being damaged by enemy action, October 1944
Source: Merseyside Maritime Museum

"You'd even be working down the hatches when they started to load the cargo, and then you'd have that to look out for, mind you didn't get hit by it. You took some risks." George Conroy recalls a couple of occasions when his life was imperilled while fitting equipment to the top of a mast to attach a barrage balloon. On one occasion he was left clinging to a mast headlight for over an hour, after the rope used to hoist him up in the bosum's chair had broken:

"During the war, you didn't bother with anything like that. You had to think of what other people were doing. There were plenty of incidents where safety could have been improved. Quite often you were working in the dark. Ships came in and had to be got ready to go out. If she was going in a convoy she had to be ready."

There were also the grave dangers of air raids, both at home and at work:

"We had some very hazardous times during the war, it was a very very fraught time, bombs dropping all over the place, incendiary bombs going off here, there and everywhere. High explosives going, blackouts, working day and night 7 days a week... There were always thousands of incendiary bombs when there was a raid on, just like snow flakes coming down, setting fire to everywhere. Everybody had a stirrup pump, as soon as you saw an incendiary bomb you'd dash out and put it out, spray it or beat it out with something."

In the workshops, to begin with, when the sirens went everyone trooped off to the air-raid shelters, but later spotters were placed on the roof so that the men could continue at work until enemy planes were within range. Men would also work up until the last minute out on the ships in a raid, which could be highly dangerous. As Tom Hartley recalls:

"We'd just got off the Elstree Grange in Hornby Dock, and down this passageway on the quay, when there was an unearthly smash. Gerry had dropped one, right down the funnel of the Elstree Grange, blew her inside out, poor old donkeyman below was killed. We wanted to go back, but the foreman said there's nothing to go back for, its blown the insides out. I had a drink after that, I'll tell you."

The worst incident of this kind was on the night of May 2nd, 1941, during the 'May Blitz'. The S.S. Malakand, with 1,000 tons of shells and bombs on board was set alight and exploded: Parts of the ship's plates were found over 2½ miles away. Howson's workshops were badly damaged in the explosion. During the May Blitz Grayson's Sandhills works were badly damaged, but remarkably back in full production by September of that year. Brown's shops lost all their windows in the Malakand explosion, but otherwise escaped largely unscathed.

Dutch ship the *Europa* hit and sunk by enemy action while in Brocklebank graving dock, during the Second World War
Source: 'The Port at War'

Apart from the risk of accidents, ship repairers also faced the possibility of long-term damage to their health from their working environment. The most common occupational hazard was deafness. Both on the ships and in the workshops the noise could be intense. Though most trades could be affected, the boilermakers seem to have suffered most. As George Conroy recalls:

> "You always used to regard the boilermakers as being deaf. Most boilermakers were slightly deaf, because you've got to remember that they were mainly concerned with riveting ships plates together, and riveting is a noisy job."

Only in the last twenty years or so have workers been provided with ear muffs or other protection. In 1963 legislation was passed which enabled workers to claim compensation. As a foremen welder remarks, it isn't only boilermakers who have claimed:

> "When a welder goes and claims deafness through working in a shipyard, they look at him and think, how daft, but its the noise from the other people. If you've got a riveter working on the hull and your working inside, its terrible."

It may come as a surprise that one of the biggest occupational hazards that ship repairers faced and are still facing, is asbestosis. There is always a great deal of asbestos around ships engines and boilers, and in the early years safety precautions were minimal or non-existent. All those who worked in a ship's engine room—engineers, fitters, boilermakers, plumbers, coppersmiths, scalers and labourers—ran the danger of exposure to asbestos dust:

> "For years and years fellas used to go and work in asbestos, just strip it down. You'd go in a ship's engine room and it used to be like snow. Taking lagging of pipes, they're going to replace the pipes or whatever, and the people down below are getting covered in this stuff."

> "I worked with asbestos for years, knee deep in it on ships at times. We'd be working in the engine room, lagging pipes. When you knocked off at night you used to go on the deck and get a compressed air line, blow one another down, blow it all off!"

But at the time workers were not aware of the dangers:

> "There was no attempt to control it, none at all. It was all over the place. When it got wet it was like a white slime. There was no control, but you didn't realise it, it didn't enter your head that this was a dangerous product. You were familiar with these things so you didn't treat them as a danger."

The worst affected were the laggers, whose job it was to remove the asbestos from pipes etc., and who came under the foreman scaler. Something of the dangers appears to have been known by the employers even in the 1920's and 30's as the laggers got slightly higher wages than scalers. Some of the white dust dislodged when removing lagging would be powdered magnesium, but this was also a health hazard.

Asbestos is still widely used on ships today, but safety standards have been revolutionised. However, this was only after the facts had become available to trade unions and their members, who pressed for change. Tragically, for many, these precautions came too late. Many ship repairers have died of asbestosis, many others have had to have a lung removed. In the early days many who had asbestosis were diagnosed as suffering from T.B. Once the dangers became widely known in the 1960's, and Health and Safety legislation made it easier to claim compensation, claims began to flood in. A former safety officer at CBS recalls dealing with hundreds of these cases in the 1970's, passing on information to insurance companies as to whether company records showed that the man had worked with asbestos at A & R Brown, as far back as the 1930's.

Many ship repairers, particularly plumbers, faced the danger of working with lead. Burners and welders would breathe in lead fumes when working in areas of a ship which were painted with red lead. No masks were issued; some men put a wet handkerchief over their face. Welders also faced the long-term health risks of a softening of chest bones and of the forehead bone. The 'flashes' they endured could also damage their eyes permanently in the long-term. All trades that used mechanical vibrating machinery could contract Reynard's Phenomena, or 'white finger' as it is commonly known. The nerves in the hands are damaged, the fingers eventually becoming numb. Many trades were prone to chest illnesses, particularly the scalers: "I had a lot of bronchial trouble when I was young. You were working in damp conditions, and sometimes you were working with your feet in water". Moulders had perhaps the most dangerous job of all. They faced the grave danger of burns from the molten metal; there was the problem of lung disease from breathing in dust from the silica sand; certain chemicals in some moulding sands were found to be carcinogenic; some suffer from arthritis due to lifting heavy weights. In the early days many suffered with ulcers on their legs from the sand: "one man got so bad he had to have a leg off".

There is a general feeling among ship repairers that, until the 1960's and 1970s, when government legislation forced them to act, the employers were negligent in their concern for safety: "They weren't worried about your health in those days as long as you were working". First-aid provision was primitive and the firms showed little or no concern over the long-term occupational hazards. Given the large number of serious accidents both on the ships and in the workshops until recent years, it is clear that general safety regulations were inadequate. Nor, until recent years, was much in the way of protective clothing provided. In the early days welders had to provide their own leather hats, gloves and shoulder protection. Protective helmets, weather cloaks and torches were only given to electricians in the 1960's after shop stewards had fought long and hard for them. Both the boilermakers' and moulders' unions were determined campaigners for adequate protective clothing, often without the full support of the membership. As Ernie Parker of the moulders' union explains,

"The foundry workers' union was a good crusading union for health and safety. The trouble with a lot of workers, not just in foundries, but in all industries, is that they think another shilling an hour protects them better than the health and safety. If they're doing a dirty job that's going to injure their health they'd sooner fight for a shilling an hour more to do that job, than say to the boss no, we're not doing that".

The moulders' union has fought for (and won) the case for compensation for deafness, white finger, and other occupational hazards.

In the event of an accident, the compensation paid to a workman or his family was often minimal. A case might involve lengthy and expensive court proceedings, though trade union members would have the backing of their union. Mr. John Gray has sent me documents concerning the death of his father, Charles Gray, as a result of blood poisoning in August 1932, apparently caused by an injury received while working for Grayson's, in Birkenhead in November 1929. He left a widow and two young sons. Eventually, in September 1933 Grayson's, while repudiating liability, agreed to pay £200 compensation.

Cammell Laird had their own way of covering themselves from having to pay compensation, as a coppersmith recalls of an accident he had during the war:

"I was working on a submarine on the docks and they were boring the shaft out of the propeller. The boring gear was a motor with gearing cogs. This was in the winter and it was very cold. I was working with a coppersmith, and I had my coat on over my overalls, it was that cold this day. Someone started up this machinery, and my coat must have been hanging over the two cogs, so it pulled me in, didn't it. In-between me getting pulled back and him seeing what had happened, and him running across the road to switch the machinery off, it tore all my clothes up to my neck. When it was to the neck I started to go round it, didn't I? It was just starting to strangle me when the machinery stopped. I fainted then.

That must have only been thirty seconds, but to me it was a lifetime going through that, I thought I was going to die.

When I came round I was in the ambulance room in Cammell Laird's, and they were saying 'come on son . . . you're alright now, not too bad, sign this'. I was still confused, they put a pen in my hand, sign there, so I signed it, I declared that there was no responsibility on the firm's part. There should have been a guard on that machinery, the guard had been taken off, but before I was off that ship that guard was on, someone whipped it on. Do you know how much I got? My back was only cut with the cogs and strained a bit but I was in shock. I got a fortnight off and my wages, the princely sum of five shillings a week. When it happened, when they let me sit down for half an hour, from the minute of that accident my pay stopped: 'You're alright son, go home for the rest of the day'. This was just after dinner. They got all my clothes and they pinned them down my back where they'd torn. Go home they said.

My father tried to do all sorts about it. I went to the doctor and he said I had delayed shock. But I just got five pounds for my clothes. That was my compensation, five pounds, and two weeks wages at five shillings a week".

THE

CRICHTON

MERSEY

SHIP REPAIRING SERVICE

6. Growth and Decline of the Industry

The development of the ship repair industry on Merseyside has always been uneven, reflecting the upward and downwards swings in trade which have been a feature of the history of the port. War has also been an important determinant of the fortunes of the industry. There was naturally plenty of work in ship repair during the First World War, and immediately after in converting ships back from military use. As Edward Bowyer recalls, "Very nearly all the cargo ships had been stripped down the hold, to carry horses to France". However, the boom gave way within a few years to the slump which gripped Britain's economy in general. By 1923 34 per cent of shipbuilding and ship repair workers on Merseyside were unemployed. Hardship was so great that many men were seriously physically weakened by lack of food when unemployed:

> "When it started again and they wanted the men, they just collapsed. They hadn't done anything, no work, no money, oh,—hard times—and when they started work again they just couldn't do it, just collapsed on the job".

The depression in ship repair naturally worsened with the dramatic slump in British and world trade from 1929. The world economy, led by the American, had overheated, business capitalising on the apparent boom, but in reality creating a surplus of goods for which there was insufficient demand. This crisis of speculation and over-production led to the Wall Street Crash, and a collapse of industrial production and trade around the world, throwing millions out of work. Thousands of Merseyside's dockside workers were thrown on the dole. The shipbuilders and ship repairers were particularly badly affected: by 1932 56 per cent were out of work. Leslie I'Anson recalls that in the early 1930's even the most highly skilled fitters were desperate for a job:

> "Some of them used to stand at the other side of the road, up against the railway wall, and the foreman would go out and pick perhaps 2 men out of 50. Some of those men had extra chief engineer's tickets, very highly qualified men, and they'd have their overalls under their arm. And they were grateful for half a day's work".

Tom Hartley remembers his own search for work at this time:

> "I remember I used to walk along the dock road from one end to the other, calling at various firms, 'come back tomorrow', you'd go back, and back, and back. It wasn't just morning, it was morning and afternoon. Morning, nothing doing. Dinnertime, nothing doing. And it could go on sometimes for weeks on end. You wore your soles out looking for a job... Could be twelve months, never mind a few weeks... We used to get 17 bob (85p) a week off the dole, we used to get by. You had to, didn't you?"

Those with a steady job and a steady wage were seen as highly fortunate. A shipwright recalls the reaction when he got a secure job as carpenter for a stevedorage firm: "My wages then were £3 9s 8d a week, that's in 1937, which was fantastic. When I got married to my wife her mother thought she was marrying the Aga Khan or something, £3 9s 8d and besides that we used to get two 9 o'clocks each week, overtime we had to do".

Such was the effect on the firms of the slump that Harland and Wolff tried to sell off their Liverpool works in February 1931, offering it as suitable for conversion into a motor vehicle repair shop. However, no buyer could be found for such large premises. Another large local firm converted part of its workshops for the refitting of road vehicles, and all the firms took "any work they could find, whether connected with shipping or not".

It is sad to say that it took another war to bring full employment. John Thompson, cost clerk at A & R Brown, recalls the changes when war was declared:

> "Being the ripe age of 21 I registered right away amongst the 21s. I had a medical examination in October and

Works' outing of Grayson Rollo, 1936. William 'Billy' Briant is holding the accordian
Loaned by Mrs. D. Briant

passed A1. But I wasn't called up until the 17th January 1940, 3 months after the start of the war, so I was able to see the change in Brown's at the beginning of the war. The work they got was transforming trawlers, which came down from Fleetwood, into minesweepers. The first trawler we did was called the Marsona. We fitted admiralty guns on the foredeck, akak guns and machine guns on the bridge and what they call a degousing cable right round the hull on the water level. When this was energised from the generators on the ship, it prevented the magnetic mines from coming up and exploding under the vessel".

George Conroy recalls how the war affected his work as a blacksmith:

"I worked mainly in the works up until 1938-39. When things were starting to warm up with the war breaking out I went to work outside. We got into a squad for fitting out ships with guns. All ships going to sea during the war had to be armed, and of course that was a major job. All ships were fitted with a gun on the stern end, on the poop.

The various decks below that all had to be stiffened up with forged stancheons. We had to make a platform for the people who were working on the guns to attend to it, and all the rails round had to be portable so that when they were in action they just dropped out".

George's squad also fitted rocket launchers, an attachment to the top of the mast to hold a barrage balloon, and apparatus for fitting paravanes, the torpedo-shaped devices towed from the bow of a vessel so that the cables cut the anchors of any moored mines.

The end of the war, far from reducing the amount of ship repair work, actually led to an increase. During the war only essential repairs had been carried out. Ships which had been requisitioned by the government in the war and converted for military use, had to be reconverted back. The Government paid for all this. This led to a great deal of work on passenger liners, as John Rock recalls: "For a while, places like A & R Brown, Harland and Wolff, the Cunard Company, made the most superb furniture you could lay your hands on. I dread to think what the cost was. An easy chair took nearly a fortnight to do!" Merseyside's ship repair firms also benefitted from the post-war boom in shipbuilding, as George Conroy of A & R Brown explains:

"After the war all the shipping companies had to have a programme of building new ships. Wherever the ship was being built, whether it was in Cammell Laird, or in Harland and Wolff in Ireland, or up in Scotland, or on the north-east coast, we'd get sub-contractor's work. We had men permanently based up there, sending back sketches of insulation work that they wanted. We would make it and send it up there. That work kept us really busy for about twelve years or so after the war".

There were over 20,000 ship repairers on Merseyside at the height of the boom in the early 1950's. A foreman welder at Grayson's remembers that "at the peak of the work I said to one of my chargehands, I've got 498 men, I'll start two men in the morning and I'll make the 500, I think I've made the record!" 500 in just one trade at one firm. "I remember the managing director one time giving us a lecture to say that it was the largest ship repair company not in the country, but the world". In the fifties, a small firm like Cubbin's employed 250 regular men, taking on many more on a more casual basis.

The prosperity of the firms in this period was exemplified by the improvements made by A & R Brown to their rather antiquated workshops and machinery, which George Conroy remembers well:

"In 1954 they closed the smithy on Regent Road and built a new smithy in Fulton Street, with modern fires and all the latest up-to-date equipment. Instead of steam hammers we had compressed air hammers fitted. We still had the same type of fire although they were a more modern design. The smithy was fitted out with new equipment, special benches for welding purposes, a special room where the welding apparatus was, everyone was fitted out with burning equipment, the forging side of the work was gradually being eroded. The Regent Road works were completely modernised. The machine shop was extended into what used to be the blacksmiths shop. The brass finishers department up on the first balcony had new machines fitted. The tin shop which was on the third floor was fitted out with new equipment. The boiler shop on Fulton Street next to the smithy was fitted with new sheers and rollers".

Two trawlers used as minesweepers in the war being reconverted back to civilian use, number five dry dock, Cammell Laird, June 1945
Source: Liverpool Daily Post and Echo

As part of the same period expansion, in 1960 Grayson's opened their new No. 1 Graving dock in Birkenhead, capable of handling vessels of up to 65,000 tons; Cammell Laird opened the largest privately owned dry dock in Britain the following year.

Such improvements in facilities were grounded on the assumption that the industry would continue to expand indefinitely. On the contrary, from about 1957 there was a significant fall off in work. Partly this was because all the repair and reconversion work consequent of the war had finally dried up. It was also a period which saw the beginnings of all those trends which were to lead to the dramatic decline of both Britain's maritime supremacy and of Liverpool's standing within the hierarchy of British ports.

Firms like Grayson's now had to 'tout' for work in a way they had never had to before:

"They got up to all kinds of tricks to get work off various shipping companies ... If a ship's captain wanted to go wrestling the ship manager on that ship would take him. Or if he wanted to go to a nightclub or a dance, or maybe he wanted a bit of female company, it would be supplied for him".

For a time firms such as Grayson's staved off the worst effects of the decline in ship repair by diversifying into other kinds of work, such as boiler repairs and general maintenance at local engineering firms. However, there was a limit to the general engineering work firms like Grayson's could find, and their payroll began to fall sharply:

"Then you had to struggle. It got to the point where the firm didn't want to keep the men on because there was no work, but you could see that there would be work in three or four days. They wouldn't even keep the men on for one day, you had to sack them and then start them a day or so later. Terrible. And then you'd knock them off for a week and then start them for a week, knock them off for a month, start them for a couple of days. That's the way it went on until eventually we just couldn't give them jobs ... When the end came you'd start two men and say 'I've only got a day's work but I'll try and give you two', to make it worth their while, but sometimes it didn't happen. We went down from 200 squads of welders rapidly to 50 ... When I left in 1961 there were two squads of welders, a squad in the workshop and a squad outside".

Fortunately this was a period of relatively high employment on Merseyside, and it seems that most of the men laid off did find work elsewhere:

> "They were finding work. They were going to Cammell Laird's and the refineries, Shell at Ellesmere Port was building up just then. They didn't like the work they were doing, there was greater freedom on the docks. Suddenly to have four walls round you in a factory wasn't very nice, they weren't used to it. They were closed in, and they were used to a lot of fresh air, but they found work".

A number of shipwrights left the industry for the new Ford factory at Halewood, attracted by higher wages.

Such was the effect of the slump on Grayson's that in October 1961 they were bought out by Cammell Laird: "I finished in October '61 and I think for three months before that we hardly had a job, little bits that you wouldn't have looked at in the old days, we would have said take it to another firm". A foreman recalls his surprise:

> "One day the managing director came to me and said 'you're going to Cammell Laird next week!' I said 'why, what's on over there?' Cammell Laird had bought Grayson Rollo's out. 'That's it, this place is finished, we're just sending all the staff over'... I remember one of the pep talks the director gave us. He said Grayson's has been in existence 200 years, there's no reason why it shouldn't be in existence another 200".

This foreman chose to leave ship repair rather than join Laird's finding work in engineering, a decision he does not regret:

> "I've met chaps since who had been sent over to Cammell Laird from there. They weren't wanted, and they didn't know how to get rid of them without causing a fuss... The foreman boilermaker, Gerald Griffin, Gerry we used to call him, he went to Laird's after Grayson Rollo closed. He ended up dishing the tea out on the decks of the ships, morning and afternoon, tea-man. They were all mocking him and he said its my pension, if I leave I've lost my pension! This is the way the employers... I sometimes lay in bed of a night and wonder why I'm not a communist, the things I've seen... Cammell Laird had obviously seen an opportunity to acquire the graving docks, thats' all they were after, the graving docks at the other side of the river, right next door to them—asset stripping isn't it?"

Grayson's impressive works at Sandhills were later closed and have since been demolished.

Grayson's were not the only firm to go to the wall at this time. Rutherford's in Birkenhead closed in January 1962, as Amy Beattie recalls:

> "I just had my fortnight's notice, then they were going to close the yard ... I got nothing after 19 years. There was no redundancy pay then".

All the ship repair firms were feeling the pinch at this time. Both A & R Brown and Crichton's were laying off large numbers of men, as Charlie Whiteside remembers:

> "When I joined A & R Brown (1957) I reckon we had about 600 men. Crichton's said they had about 1500 and then eventually they went down to about 800 and A & R Brown were down eventually to about 250 ... At one stage it was down to 40. In the boilermakers' department there were only the foreman and 4 boilermakers who were all shop stewards".

Merseyside ship repairers took part in this march to a mass lobby of Parliament to protest against rising unemployment, organised by Liverpool Trades Council, in November 1962
Loaned by Jack McAllister

Then early in 1963 the two firms announced an amalgamation. This came as a great shock, as Ken Patterson recalls:

"You could see the gradual easing off of work but nobody was doing any panicking. Then all of a sudden little rumours, they were getting taken over, and it was getting called Crichton Brown, not Brown & Crichton, Crichton Brown. Oh blimey, Crichton's must have bought Brown's, but how could they?"

Once the amalgamation was announced, many Brown's men were sacked, including Ken Patterson:

"Some were taken over to Crichton's, some were just thrown out on the scrap heap. I got a week's notice which was very unusual, all the rest got 2 hour's notice. Sacked in 2 hours, and in 2 hours all your pay and overtime and everything would be ready for you... The likes of me were saying 'well, what the hell do I do?' Been working here for 20 odd years, 22 years, and what do I do now? I was married, a family growing up, so there was resentment, but I think we were more scared than anything else, because jobs then were starting on the decline for pattern makers".

Probably over half of Brown's men were sacked, whereas the Crichton's men were all kept on, which led many to feel that it was not a merger but a takeover. Brown's men seem to have got a raw deal at the new firm: 'after a few months people were getting stopped and stopped and it was all Brown's men'; 'within a year or eighteen months of them merging' most of the Brown's men 'had been whittled out'. Fortunately most of the ex-Brown's men were able to find jobs elsewhere, mostly outside ship repair.

At about the same time, also to stave off the worst effects of the collapse of business, Russell's and Howson's combined to form Sandhills Engineering. But the late 1960's and 1970's saw only a continued decline. The period 1965 to 1975 was a crucial one in the contraction of Britain's maritime fleet. The passenger liner all but disappeared. Containerisation came to prominence, not only cutting the number of ships, but also the amount of repair work required. Voyage repairs and planned maintenance were also developed. The second rank of world trading nations, such as India and Nigeria, developed their own fleets, in direct competition with the British. The world energy crisis at the end of the period produced a slump in world trade, which further drastically cut Britain's merchant shipping.

Liverpool and Birkenhead suffered more than most British ports from the changes of this period. Containerisation replaced the cargo liner, on which Merseyside's prominence within Britain was based, and the port was particularly unsuited to containerisation. Merseyside was not well placed to benefit from the rapid expansion of bulk oil, gas and chemical carriers before the oil crisis. Britain's entry into Europe in 1973 probably hit Liverpool harder than any other port in the country.

As a result of this slump, in 1972 Crichton Brown and Sandhills Engineering amalgamated to form CBS Engineering. In 1978 Western Ship Repairers, as Cammell Laird's repair facilities were by then known, were closed. The workers put up a brave, but ultimately unsuccessful fight against closure, occupying the yard for over two years. The 1970s saw a steady decline in the volume of work at CBS also. According to Ted Seddon, "they were getting slacker and slacker, you used to go to work, and they'd say 'there's no work, go home'—you were on call". When closure came in May 1980, it was perhaps not unexpected, but the men were given little notice:

"We said to the steward 'whose going home today?' He said 'I want you all in a meeting, you're all going home', and that's the last we heard, the firm was finished. We even clubbed together to send shop stewards down to parliament to lobby them to see if they could get some ships up, but it was no good, it was finished".

He recalls his last day:

"Terrible, oh it was heartbreaking. The day we finished, I came out and I sat in the car, and I must have sat there for half an hour on my own, just saying '41 years, finished'. It hit me like a ton of bricks".

There were no big redundancy payments either. One man recalls that for over 40 years service "I got £2 short of two thousand five hundred quid".

The closure of CBS was especially bitter because there was little chance of getting another job in the industry. Bob Morrison got five weeks at Archibald Brown; a few others went to a small new firm, Seaforth Welding, but this has since closed. With so few jobs going, there is a feeling that working conditions have returned to the way they were in the 1930's:

"I worked quite recently at Seaforth welding, and there they were going back to the old days in regard to stopping and starting. I m not saying we didn't get paid well, but

March in protest against the closure of Western Ship Repairers, 1978
Source: Liverpool Daily Post and Echo

they got their pound of flesh, because as soon as a job was finished you were sacked, even if it meant that night. Between ships they'd have all hands then, something I'd never thought I'd see: a boilermaker picking a brush and shovel up. I've never seen boilermakers so frightened in all my life as when I saw them at Seaforth Welding".

Many ship repairers have been unable to find any work since 1980. Others have had to take all kinds of low status jobs. Some, such as Bob Morrison and Jack Chester, were able to get jobs as attendants at the Maritime Museum, their own working lives already part of the history of the port. Bob Morrison recalls taking his grandson on a tour of the docks:

"My grandson said 'Oh grandad, I wish I'd been here when all the ships were here'. I said 'you don't think I'd be working in the Maritime Museum if the ships were here, I'd be doing my own job".

The startling collapse of the industry has left behind a great residue of highly skilled workers—whose years of training and experience do not guarantee them a job. Some keep up their skills in doing favours for friends or charity work. John Rock, upholsterer:

"I decided that I was going to start putting my skills and the things I'd learnt years ago, some cases 40 years ago, back into practice. And I did. I wanted to do what they call a chaise longue. When I was an apprentice if somebody had offered me a chaise longue to upholster, I'd have run screaming out the door. But all the things that these old men had taught me so many years before came back!"

Gone for good, however, are Bob Morrison's hopes that his three grandsons could in turn serve their time in the industry. Merseyside's ship repairers now mourn the passing of an industry which was still in its heyday little more than thirty years ago. John Thompson remembers A & R Brown with affection:

"We still have a look, Joyce and I, when we come along the dock road by car, we slow down and have a look. I've even been round the back and had a poke round, having a look where this was and trying to recognise where that was. It's very nostalgic. The Convivial pub is still on the corner. Where Brown's was is now a car park, but it you look at the wall you can see where the chimney breast comes up, the fireplace. I know the exact spot against the wall where we used to sit by the fireplace, you can picture it, even though the building is gone".

This nostalgia is tinged with bitterness. There is also a lack of a clear understanding as to why the industry has declined so dramatically. Such confusion is not surprising, given the great range of factors that have led to the decline: changes in shipping design, technology and organisation; global economic developments and crises; the consequent collapse of the British maritime industry; and the ways in which these global and national changes have had a greater impact on Merseyside than other British ports. It is through this complex web of factors that one can comprehend the sudden collapse of the ship repair industry; and not in the media myths of a militant and strike-bound Merseyside.

Docklands History Books

Other titles available

If you have enjoyed this book, you may be interested in the three other books in this series, available from all good local bookshops.

'The Liverpool Docklands—Life and Work in Athol Street' — Pat Ayers £2.95

> "If they knock all this down it'll be like when they flooded all those ancient monuments in Egypt to build that dam. Everything'll be swept away, not just the buildings, everything that goes with it . . . and you can't help but ask yourself what it was all about?"

This book attempts to capture the lives of the people who lived and worked in the Liverpool docklands. It uses the words and photographs of the people themselves to uncover the reality of life in a dockland community and how this changed over time.

'The Tapestry Makers' — Alan Johnson & Kevin Moore £1.95

This is the unique story of the tapestry makers of Birkenhead. Lee's Tapestry Works produced beautiful tapestries and embroideries which were exported all over the world. Many luxury liners of the 1930s, such as the Queen Mary, were furnished with Lee's fabrics. This book tells the history of the women and men who worked at Lee's from its opening in 1908 to its closure in 1970.

'Working the Tides' — Alan Johnson £2.95

> "It was a world of its own. A world within a world. Not at all like a factory or industrial complex. It was unique."

> "Well, you can imagine bombs whistling and screaming through the air, incendiaries falling and bursting all over the place . . . There was no question of going into a shelter. Time and tide waits for no man, particularly the tide."

These are just two of the many memories recalled in the book. In it you will read about the world of the Harbour Masters Department of the Mersey Docks and Harbour Board. You will learn of the men who 'worked the tides' and brought the ships in and out of the Port of Liverpool.